Simply Christians

Simply Christians

The Lives and Message of the Blessed Martyrs of Tibhirine

Thomas Georgeon and François Vayne

Preface
Cardinal Giovanni Angelo Becciu

Translated by Daniel B. Gallagher

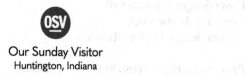

Our Sunday Visitor
Huntington, Indiana

Published in English by Our Sunday Visitor Publishing Division, Our
Sunday Visitor Inc., 200 Noll Plaza, Huntington, IN 46750; 1-800-348-
2440; www.osv.com.

ISBN: 978-1-68192-623-0 (Inventory No. T2485)
1. RELIGION—Christianity—Saints & Sainthood.
2. BIOGRAPHY & AUTOBIOGRAPHY—Religious.
3. RELIGION—Christianity—Catholic.

eISBN: 978-1-68192-624-7
LCCN: 2020941060

Cover design: Amanda Falk
Cover art: Adobe Stock
Interior design: Lindsey Riesen

PRINTED IN THE UNITED STATES OF AMERICA

*"Christian triumph is always a cross,
yet a cross which is at the same time
a victorious banner
borne with aggressive tenderness
against the assaults of evil."*

— Pope Francis, *Evangelii Gaudium*, 85

TABLE OF CONTENTS

PREFACE
Cardinal Angelo Becciu   9

INTRODUCTION
Pilgrims of Friendship and Universal Brotherhood   13

THE CONTEXT
A Panoramic View of the History of the Algerian Church   19

CHAPTER 1
Called to Make a Gift of Self in the Little Things of the Everyday   39

CHAPTER 2
Praying Together, in the Church   47

CHAPTER 3
Working in the Fruitful Silence of Nazareth   55

CHAPTER 4
Overcoming a Chain of Crises through a Series of Rebirths   63

CHAPTER 5
Living in a New Spirit of Dialogue and Cooperation   71

CHAPTER 6
Accepting the Unexpected with Mary   79

CHAPTER 7
Guests in the House of Islam   89

APPENDIX 1
Spiritual Testimony of Father Christian   99

APPENDIX 2
The Spirit of Tibhirine is Alive (Interview with
Brother Jean-Pierre Schumacher)   103

NOTES   109

PREFACE

"**N**o one has greater love than this, to lay down one's life for one's friends" (Jn 15:13).

Among the myriad holy men and women depicted on the walls of the Vatican's *Redemptoris Mater* Chapel commissioned by Saint John Paul II, we find the prior of the Tibhirine Cistercian community, Father Christian de Chergé. This is but one example of the inspiration this extraordinary Christian witness has given to artists, writers, composers, sculptors, actors, and theologians who have turned to this simple monk and his six companions, all of whom were martyred in Algeria. Millions more have been deeply moved by the award-winning film entitled *Des hommes et des dieux* (*Of Gods and Men*) by Xavier Beauvois.

Aside from the example of their heroic self-sacrifice, what can these twentieth-century martyrs teach us about the Church's common journey in this world — the journey of those who have heard a call to be "simply Christian," just like the monks of Tibhirine?

This is the question proposed by Giulio Cesareo, general editor of the Vatican publishing house *Libreria Editrice Vaticana*, whom I thank for coming up with the idea for this book. It was he who first spoke about the project with journalist François

Vayne, who, in turn, recalled that he knew something about the Tibhirine community from his childhood in North Africa. Vayne diligently dug up memories and agreed to collaborate with Father Thomas Georgeon, postulator of the nineteen beatification causes in Algeria — including the seven Cistercian monks — in writing this book. Each brought a unique experience and expertise to these meditations on the human and spiritual journey of these monastic brothers.

Each chapter takes up the story of one of the seven brothers, focusing on some particular aspect of a single spiritual mystery: "No one has greater love than this, to lay down one's life for one's friends" (Jn 15:13). This is because, in effect, Christian, Christophe, Luc, Michel, Célestin, Paul, and Bruno did not choose to be martyrs; they had only chosen to love! "They did not flee from violence. They fought it with the weapons of love, friendly hospitality, and common prayer," Pope Francis said in a preface to a historic book appearing twenty years after the martyrs' death (Christophe Henning, *Tibhirine, L'héritage* [Montrouge: Bayard, 2016]).

The leader of the community, Father Christian de Chergé — referring to a quote from Saint Maximilian Kolbe, a Catholic priest in Auschwitz who offered his life in place of a married layman and father — spoke about a "martyrdom of love." The Trappist community expressed this love in a thoroughly "incarnate" way by cultivating a relationship with their Muslim neighbors. We can also think of it as a "martyrdom of brotherhood": a real solidarity, especially during a time of extreme violence.

Under the spiritual guidance of their prior, the brothers of the Atlas Abbey were, above all, contemplative monks. During their General Chapter, Pope Francis reminded members of the Cistercian Order of the Strict Observance that "to be a contemplative means you undertake a faithful journey to become men and women of prayer, filled with greater love for the Lord and transformed into his friends. ... In this way, you become teachers and witnesses who offer Him a sacrifice of praise as you intercede for the needs and the salvation of His people. At the same time, your monasteries will always be privileged places where you can discover the true peace and genuine happiness that only God, our 'Safe Haven,' can give" (September 23, 2017).

Do we share this deep sense of service? Do we believe that our acts of charity toward God and neighbor have infinite weight? "All those who entrust themselves to God in love will bear good fruit," Pope Francis wrote in *Evangelii Gaudium* (279). "This fruitfulness is often invisible, elusive and unquantifiable. We can know quite well that our lives will be fruitful, without claiming to know how, or where, or when."

The community at Tibhirine offers the Church a resounding message, inviting us to place the spiritual realm at the center of every action we take in our families, our societies, and the world. This spiritual "irrigation" of life in all its dimensions is the gift that these Trappist brothers — these "simple Christians" — have left us.

The Church has never had a greater need to rediscover the mystical dimension of her being, to come out of herself by starting with the things above, serving others precisely within the purview of eternity, in light of the resurrection promised to us.

Cardinal Angelo Becciu
Prefect for the Congregation for the Causes of Saints
Rome, September 14, 2018
Feast of the Exaltation of the Cross

INTRODUCTION

Pilgrims of Friendship and Universal Brotherhood

T he work of discernment is never easy. The bishops of the four dioceses in Algeria erupted in an exclamation of joy on January 27, 2018, when Pope Francis authorized the Congregation for the Causes of Saints to promulgate the decree of beatification for Bishop Pierre Claverie and eighteen men and women religious companions assassinated between May 1994 and August 1996. The seven Trappist monks of the monastery in Tibhirine were among them.

"We have been given the grace of remembering our nineteen religious brothers and sisters who gave their lives in the greatest witness of love: as martyrs for those whom they loved," they wrote. "Despite the danger of death that spread throughout the country," the martyrs-to-be chose "to live fully the bond of brotherhood and friendship they had built with their brothers and sisters in Algeria for the sake of love," bonds that were "stronger than their fear of death."

The Algerian bishops were eager to unite the entire country in honoring those who had died, including 114 imams who had also been assassinated. They wrote that these men and women "had no fear of risking their lives to maintain their fidelity to God, to country, and to conscience. Our brothers and sisters would not tolerate being separated from the women and men for whom they gave their lives. They stand as witnesses of a brotherhood without borders, a love without prejudice. This is the reason their death signifies the martyrdom of countless Algerians, Muslims, people in search of meaning, workers for peace, persecuted for the cause of justice, men and women of an upright heart who had remained faithful even to the point of death during that bleak and bloody decade in Algeria."

"These beatifications," they continued, "tell us that hate is never an appropriate response to hate, and that there is no such thing as a hopeless vortex of violence. ... They represent a step toward pardon and peace for all humankind, starting with Algeria and going far beyond. They utter a prophetic word to the entire world." If, finally, many have questioned and continue to question the Church's presence in Algeria, should not the vocation of that local Church be, in fact, to prophesy to the universal Church? The Algerian Church has chosen to make her number one priority the cultivation of brotherly and friendly relations as the privileged way of expressing the essence of Christian faith and service. She now offers us nineteen examples of that kind of holiness: "Our brothers and sisters are, in the end, models of the journey toward ordinary holiness," the Algerian bishops wrote, adding that they show us that "a simple life — albeit one totally given to God and to neighbor — can carry us to the apex of the human vocation."

As members of a tiny church made up mostly of foreigners, Sister Paul-Helen and Brother Henri Vergès, Sister Esther and Sister Caridad, the four White Fathers of Cabilia, Sister Bibiane and Sister Angela Marie, Sister Odette, the seven monks of Tibhirine and His Excellency Bishop Claverie saw clearly that "when you love somebody you do not abandon that person when put to the test." These martyrs evoke for us "the daily miracle of friendship and brotherhood. ... Many of us knew them personally and lived among them. Now their life belongs to all. Now they accompany us as pilgrims of friendship and universal brotherhood," showing us a new road for interreligious dialogue, probably because the most beautiful transformations occur precisely in the midst of tragic circumstances.

Pilgrims of friendship and universal brotherhood, pilgrims of the God who is eternal love: This is what the Trappist monks were in an extraordinary way by means of their communal, spiritual journey next to their Muslim neighbors in a small, isolated village called Tibhirine, situated at an altitude of nearly 3,300 feet above sea level, not far from the city of Medea in the southwestern part of Algeria. The monastery possessed the one bell that still rang in Algeria, a place where Christians and Muslims lived a happy dialogue about life and stood side-by-side in everyday living. These simple villagers never would have been noticed if it were not for the death of the monks which echoed throughout the world. It was their deaths that sealed their fate as martyrs, or, as the word means literally, as "witnesses": witnesses to the Christ to whom they had consecrated their entire lives, witnesses of God's love for the land of Algeria and its inhabitants, for whom they gave their lives. Their "martyrdom of love" is also a "martyrdom of hope." The film *Of Gods and Men* — which won the *Grand Prix* at the Cannes Film Festival in 2010 and the César Award for Best Film of the Year in 2011 — helped spread their message across the globe.

Although centuries later, their deaths reminds us of the Scillitan martyrs: seven men and five women put to death by the proconsul Vigellius Saturninus in Carthage on July 17, 180, and subsequently recognized as the first North African martyrs.

Loyal to the people among whom they lived and worked, the monks of Tibhirine refused to obey the official order that they leave their monastery during a bloody civil war and the so-called

Great Terror. They were abducted by a mysterious band of armed
men during the night between March 26 and 27, 1996. Their severed heads were discovered fifty-six days later, and to this day
the abductors — foreigners to the region, according to the Muslim security guards at the monastery — have not been identified
with certainty. Some seek the truth with a lowercase "t" — that is,
human truth; but there are others who seek Truth with a capital
"T" — that is, the truth that is God. "Their sacrifice has revealed
the gift God gave us in them," said the then archbishop of Algiers,
Henri Teissier, in the wake of the tragedy. "This gift has become a
sign and an invitation for us." He went on to say that "they signi-
fied that God can live among us and make us witnesses in a way
that transcends every obstacle and confession. They invite us to
allow the gift God gives each of us to bear fruit in our lives, not
only for ourselves and the Church, but for all our brothers and
sisters, regardless of religious affiliation."

These seven consecrated members of the Cistercian Order
of the Strict Observance (Trappists) — Paul, Michel, Christophe,
Célestin, Luc, Bruno, and Christian — also show us that "growth
in holiness is a journey in community," as Pope Francis wrote
in his apostolic exhortation *Gaudete et Exsultate* (On the Call to
Holiness in Today's World). "We should also remember the more
recent witness borne by the Trappists of Tibhirine, Algeria, who
prepared as a community for martyrdom," the pope exhorts, urging us to allow the grace of baptism to flourish in us, insofar as
"we are all called to be witnesses."

"The Holy Father's message and the message of the Tibhirine
martyrs is one and the same," wrote Paul Desfarges, archbishop of Algiers, in his diocesan bulletin *Rencontres* ("Encounters")
after having read *Gaudete et Exsultate*. He observed that "next-
door" holiness is precisely how we should describe the journey of
our Tibhirine brothers (cf. *Gaudete et Exsultate*, 6) and the appeal
we should make to our Church, which we might call a "next-door

Church" — that is, a Church who "leaves her door open and goes to knock on the door of her neighbors."

This book particularly aims to examine the Tibhirine brothers as "simply Christians." Their lives offer a model of holiness in our own everyday lives of simplicity, humility, and a hunger to know others. Their never-failing openness to the Other and to others spurs us on and drives us to be fraternally present to others. By their prayers of intercession, they help sustain all ecclesial communities called to be "a sacrament of encounter and friendship," a sign of the Gospel in the living spirit of Tibhirine.

Thomas Georgeon and François Vayne
Rome, August 1, 2018

THE CONTEXT

A Panoramic View of the History of the Algerian Church

The common history of Algeria, Tunisia, Morocco, and Libya is rooted in the Roman Empire's presence in North Africa. Accounts of the earliest persecutions attest to the presence of Christians in the region, especially the Scillitan martyrs in a town called Scillium on July 17, 180, and the Madaurian martyrs of the same period in an ancient Roman-Numidian city near today's Souk Ahras in Algeria.

The Church in North Africa grew rapidly. A religious man born in the region of Aurés became bishop of Rome and hence pope, known by the name of Victor I, at the end of the second century. It was during this time that Latin began to replace Greek as the liturgical language, so we can say that the seeds of Latin in the Church were planted in North Africa, thanks to the translation of the Bible and works written by Tertullian, a Berber born in Carthage. These are, in fact, the oldest Latin Christian texts.

In the middle of the fourth century, Donatus, a bishop in the region of Aurés in eastern Algeria, preached an intolerant Church, the validity of whose sacraments depended on the holiness of her ministers. Donatus was killed in 355 after having created a schismatic group against Rome. The sanctions imposed by Constantine against the powerful Donatist church weakened the Church in North Africa for some time, until Saint Augustine, the greatest Latin Church Father, came along and made a major contribution to the growth of Christianity once more, having participated in thirty or so regional and provincial councils. Born in Tagaste (Souk Ahras, Algeria) in 354, Augustine, who had been made bishop of Hippo, died in 430 during a siege of the city by a man named Geiseric, king of the Vandals. During the ideological fanaticism of the Donatists, who proudly sought death and took delight in confronting idolaters, Saint Augustine never tired of describing martyrdom as a freely accepted gift in a spirit of faith and poverty rather than an ambitious, vain, self-willed act.

The theories of Arius (256–336), a Berberist theologian from Libya, which denied the divinity of Christ, became more and more widespread after the Vandals, who were themselves Arians (442–533), occupied the area and allied themselves with the Donatist zeal against the Catholic Church.

At the time of the council in 484 there were thirty bishops in the region currently known as Algeria; but by 1076, there were none. That was the year Pope Gregory VII sent a bishop at the request of the Muslim prince En-Naçir. The bishop, Servandus, settled in Bougie after fleeing the invasions of the Banu Hilal, a confederation of Arabian tribes. The incursion of the Vandals and the feuds among Donatists, Arians, Catholics, and later Muslims resulted in a localized Latin church without its own liturgy in a Berber tongue. Furthermore, this ancient church lacked strong monasteries it could depend on, as was also the case in the Middle East.

After the domination of the Vandals (a people of Scandinavian origin) in northern Africa, and a brief period of Byzantine reconquest under Emperor Justinian, Muslim Arabs annexed the Berber lands of Maghreb (647), finding the Arian heresy fertile ground for propagating Islam. The Ottoman Turks turned Algeria into an Ottoman province in 1575; it stayed such until French troops disembarked in 1830 in Sidi Fredj, which would become French territory and remain so until 1962, when it gained independence.

With the advent of French colonization in 1830, as well as the need to rid the Mediterranean of barbarian pirates — Islamic North-Africans and Ottomans — especially beginning in Algeria, a new Church was born in Algeria. The archbishop of Algeria, Cardinal Charles Lavigerie, founded the White Fathers and White Sisters, the "Missionaries of Africa," who gave witness to the Gospel in a Muslim environment through service to the poor and teaching.

The witness of Father Charles de Foucauld, "confessor of the faith," assassinated in the Algerian desert in 1916 at Tamanrasset and beatified in Rome in 2005, as well as the two congregations that he inspired — the Little Brothers and Little Sisters of Jesus — and his large spiritual family including many laypeople, had a large influence on the relationship of the Catholic Church to members of other religions — which, in turn, contributed to the convocation of the Second Vatican Council.

After Algeria achieved independence from France in 1962, most European Christians, carrying everything on their backs, departed the country and headed for France to replant their families there. Some of these families had been living abroad for six generations. Cardinal Léon-Etienne Duval, archbishop of Algiers, exhorted the local Church to become fully Algerian by participating in the development of the nation, such as by founding centers of professional development and establishing health clinics.

An "Algerian church" specifically meant a church whose identity was precisely that of Algeria. At the end of the War of Independence in 1962, much work had to be done to rebuild the country: Education, health care, and social works of various types were precisely the areas in which Christians could collaborate with Algerian Muslims. For this reason, many church buildings, as well as churches that had fallen into disuse, were dedicated to social and educational works. Priests, religious men and women, and lay Christians easily found a niche where they could readily dedicate themselves to promoting the human good through various services. They would soon receive the help of thousands of workers (engineers, technicians, teachers, and doctors) who came to lend a hand to a country in need of full reconstruction. Initially, there was even a type of euphoria, fortified by the social ideology of Algerian politics, that promised a glorious future that many actually came to believe in.

Within this atmosphere of optimism, and to demonstrate their desire to link their own destiny with the country's, several religious men and women petitioned for Algerian citizenship in 1965 in the footsteps of the local Church's protective, paternal figure Cardinal Duval. When asked, "What is the future of the Algerian Church, given that you are not allowed to bring about any conversions?" he responded, "The future of the Church is in the hearts of Algerians."

The reality, however, was not "euphoric." There was a need to cultivate a fraternal love capable of building bridges beyond the borders of the Church. This is precisely the focal point we find in the pontificate of Francis. In Algeria, the perennial character of the Church is not to be found in its visible limits, but rather in the lively and dedicated fraternal love that Cardinal Duval talks about. The local Church sank into a deep sorrow after the knifing of Gaston Jacquier, auxiliary bishop of Algiers, in July 1976, as a new constitution proclaimed a revolution based on the spirit of Arab socialism under a single-party rule. "Arabization" was imposed, schools were nationalized, and farmlands were organized into Soviet-style cooperatives.

Father Jean-Marie Jover was assassinated in 1985. For a while, his name was connected to the nineteen Catholic victims in the years that followed (as Archbishop Teissier stated in a homily during a Mass for the twenty new martyrs on May 6, 2000, in the Church of Saint Augustine in Rome).

Continually smaller, but alive with fraternal charity, the Catholic community grew tighter around the Cistercian monastery of Tibhirine, where the brothers played a fundamental role in spiritually accompanying both Catholics and Muslims, until they were detained in 1996. Cardinal Duval called the monastery at Tibhirine a "lung" of the diocese.

Algeria fell into an Islamist crisis at the end of the 1980s. Until that time, the FLN (*Front de Libération Nationale*), which had been leading the country since it achieved independence, seemed to be in control of things. In October 1988, major revolts — at the cost of many human lives and the unbalancing of an already unbalanced social structure — erupted and spread throughout Algeria. Overcome by the rising tide of popular discontent, the regime declared a state of emergency and repressed public demonstrations with brute force. Hundreds died as a result.

Algerians abandoned their trust in the country's leaders. The leaders, in turn, frantically attempted to regain it by proposing political reforms that would allow for a multiparty system. Islamists had the most to gain from this. In an atmosphere of constant change, the Church was closer to the people than ever as she called for greater political freedom and an end to the single-party system and its privileges.

After multiple clashes in October 1988, culminating in the shooting of several university students, free elections were finally sanctioned in 1989. Some leaders of the former one-party system "played with fire," showing sympathy for the rising tide of radical Islam and aligning themselves with the Berberists. A blaze finally erupted during municipal and legislative elections in June 1990 and December 1991, in which Islamists gained the upper hand. They promised equality and social justice (having obtained 100 percent of the vote in Medea, located in Tibhirine; consequently, the city became the planned site of the new Islamic State). After the breakdown of the electoral process and the declaration of a state of emergency, Islamists in January 1992 declared war on the military, who had been in power since the time of independence from France.

"Many viewed the terrorists as defenders of the community; people who could lead a legitimate battle against injustice," explained American historian John Kiser. The Islamic Salvation Front (FIS) did its best to respect the precepts of Islam during the conflict by sparing innocent civilians, but soon various radical terrorist groups forced the country into a bloody mess.

The Algerian crisis cost between 100,000 and 150,000 lives in the 1990s. Even though the nineteen beatified martyrs received most of the attention, it is important to remember the precious lives of many others whose families are still mourning their deaths. Many were left widowed or abandoned as a result of the violence. It is important, too, to remember that only a fraction of those who died were Christians.

In the spring of 1994, Pierre Claverie, bishop of Oran, born in Algeria during the period of colonization and therefore a *"pied-noir,"* courageously spoke out against the "merciless repression" of Algeria, declaring publicly that "militant Islamists are being enflamed with the fury of ever-increasing murder." He revealed that one of the emirs of the Islamist rebellion admitted that "the Church will have a role in the society we intend to build. Don't worry. We will protect you." The martyr-to-be added that he wished to imitate Cardinal Duval in listening to the suffering of the Algerian people and the injustices against them "so that the Church's presence would remain in this country," and that he "thanks God that no one has yet been killed in Algeria because of his or her Catholicism."

A few days after this declaration, on May 8, 1994 — which happened to be the bishop's birthday — the bloody deaths of the nineteen religious men and women began. The name of the bishop would be added to that list on August 1, 1996. Addressing himself precisely to those questioning the reason for those programmatic murders, Henri Teissier, archbishop emeritus of Algiers, had this to say at a press conference in Rome on March 22, 2018: "Jesus died for political reasons, too." In a beautiful prayer composed for the processes of beatification and canonization of Bishop Claverie and his eighteen fellow martyrs (launched in Rome on October 4, 2007), Teissier wrote, "Lord, help us to remember the deaths of our brothers in such a way that, rather than renewing a time of violence and exclusion, we accept the invitation to respect one another in the courage of truth and the work of peace."

The Tibhirine Community from Its Founding till the Present Day

During negotiations with the French military in May 1837, Emir Abdelkader, the soul of the resistance during the time of French occupation, scornfully remarked to General Thomas Robert Bugeaud, commander of the French colonial army, that "Christians don't pray." The impiety of the French soldiers was, in effect, a cause for scandal to the Muslims, as numerous prisoners freed by Abdelkader had claimed in a book published at that time. General Bugeaud then suggested to the first bishop of Algiers, Antoine-Adolphe Dupuch, that he establish a monastery in Algeria for a contemplative community. This is why Trappists were suddenly called to open a monastery near Algiers, thus bestowing a name to the surrounding community: "La Trappa."

As the war against Abdelkader raged on (it would continue until 1847), fourteen Trappist monks from the Abbey of Aiguebelle arrived in Algeria in 1843. They settled in Staouéli on the western outskirts of Algiers on August 20 — the feast of Saint Bernard, the medieval abbot of Clairvaux and a Doctor of the Church. The plot of land they acquired, consisting of approximately 2,500 acres, was "buried in thorny bushes, scorched and arid, covered with miniature palm trees, and overrun by wild animals." A statue of Our Lady of Africa was placed at the entrance of the monastery and renamed "Queen of Africa" in 1856 by the new bishop of Algiers, Louis-Antoine-Augustin Pavy. It was later moved to the Marian shrine perched between the Mediterranean and "The White City." One of the most famous pilgrims to this shrine would arrive at Staouéli in September 1896: Charles de Foucauld, later known as "Brother of All," who at that time was a Trappist monk bearing the name of Brother Alberico. He came there to reflect on his vocation as a hermit.

Having dedicated 370 acres to grain and 125 acres to vine growing, the monastery quickly became an important agricultural center in Algeria. However, the separation between Church and state and the anticlerical laws of the French Republic at the beginning of the twentieth century forced the community at Staouéli into self-imposed exile in Italy, near Lago di Garda, in Maguzzano. They subsequently sold their property to Colonel Henri Borgeaud.

This exile, however, did not shake their commitment to Algeria. Some Slovenian monks at Maguzzano — together with French monks at Aiguebelle — finally returned to Algeria to rebuild the monastery in 1934, reconnecting with Brother François, the only Trappist to remain in Algeria as he awaited the arrival of others to establish a new monastic community. In 1938, after having attempted to establish a community in the south of Algeria in Ben Chicao, near Medea, the monks finally decided to settle in the same region, in the agricultural area of Tib-Harine, which in Berber means "watered gardens." They purchased this "land of Tib-Harine," consisting of around 1,235 acres, from a lawyer named Benoît Mosca (the name Tib-Harine became Tibhirine in 1962). The soil was easily irrigated and fertile.

The new abbey, entrusted to the patronage of "Our Lady of Atlas," was subject to its mother abbey of Aiguebelle, located in the French department of Drôme, from the beginning of the Cistercian presence in Algeria. On August 17, 1939, two monks went to the ancient cemetery of Staouéli and happened to find a statue of the expectant Virgin Mary with a crescent moon under her feet and wearing a crown of twelve stars, just as described in the Book of Revelation. They brought this statue back to Tibhirine and placed it on a large rock named Abd el-Kader, where it was blessed on September 8, 1939.

It was there that Brother Luc (Paul Dochier) arrived with five other monks from the Abbey of Aiguebelle in August 1946. He began working in an already existing infirmary that, lacking a doctor, was staffed by an herbalist monk.

Life in the monastery was not all smooth sailing. Members of the community from significantly different backgrounds had to find ways to live and work together. Two of the members had lived in Staouéli; others lived in a monastery in Yugoslavia; some arrived in 1938; and still others came in 1946. Various superiors succeeded one another until, on September 26, 1947, the monastery finally was granted status as an abbey. The abbot-elect, Father Barbaroux, decided to use a crosier from the Abbey of Staouéli to symbolize the historic link between the two communities.

During the Algerian War of Independence from France, between 1954 and 1962, the French army suspected the monks of offering support to the Algerian rebels by means of the doctor of the community, Brother Luc. French soldiers set the monastery's barn on fire, alleging it was used to shelter terrorists. Brother Luc and another monk by the name of Brother Mathieu were abducted in 1959 by the so-called Mujahideen fellaghas — Muslim combatants from the National Liberation Front — but they were released a few days later.

In 1962, while many Europeans were fleeing Algeria due to the atmosphere of terrorism that preceded the nation's proclamation of independence, only a few monks remained at Tibhirine. In 1963, against the will of Cardinal Duval, archbishop of Algiers, the abbot general of the Cistercian Order decreed that the monastery should be closed. However, the decree was never implemented due to the sudden death of the abbot general. Hence, it was necessary to reactivate the community. This was done through an appeal to carry out the Cistercian monastic life "in the land of Islam." Eight new members arrived in 1964 from the abbeys of Timadeuc and Aiguebelle. The Algerian authorities had stipulated that the community not number more than a dozen members. Impelled by a zeal for simplicity and humility, the monks handed over more than seven hundred acres of their property to the Algerian state, keeping about fifteen for their own use.

According to the logic of an "irreversible choice" for socialism in 1976, the government forced the collectivization of farms. The monks, who at the time labeled themselves as "people of prayer in the midst of people of prayer," grew even closer to local farmers by forming an agricultural cooperative that shared a plot of approximately twenty acres. It was in this year that they elected a superior in conformity with canon law and solidified the rules of common life.

At the urging of Claude Rault, a White Father, and Christian de Chergé, who arrived in Tibhirine in 1971, the *Ribat es Salam* — "bond of peace" — was born, a group of Muslims and Christians who met for the first time in Tibhirine in March 1979. This group came about precisely due to a desire to deepen a common spiritual life and to learn more about the religious experience of Muslims, thus allowing Christians to better live out their vocation in Algeria.

In 1984, the status of the monastery transitioned from a dependent abbey to an autonomous priory, taking the name *Notre-Dame de l'Atlas*. Brother Christian, elected prior on March 31 of that year (he would be reelected in 1990), launched an appeal for volunteers to come and help build up the Tibhirine community. Several heeded the appeal, and brothers from the Abbeys of Aiguebelle, Bellefontaine, and Tamié came to join the monastery.

In 1988, the monastic community established an "associated monastic cell" in Fez, Morocco, in response to a request from the archbishop of Rabat, Hubert Michon, for a monastic presence in that country to supplement the community of the Little Sisters of Jesus. This *dépendance* in Fez played an essential role during the years of 1993 to 1996, when violence erupted in Algeria. The brothers in Tibhirine, in fact, made numerous trips to Fez to find relief from the war in Algeria and regain their strength with the brothers living in Morocco.

In the first free, multiparty elections — first municipal in 1990, and then legislative in 1991 — the village of Tibhirine voted unanimously for Islamists, even though the local Muslim population remained tightly tied to the monks. On October 30, 1993, the Armed Islamic Group (GIA) issued an ultimatum for all foreigners to leave the country before December 1. On December 14, 1993, twelve Croatian expatriates, friends of the monastery in Tibhirine, were strangled in Tamesguida near Medea, about two and a half miles from the monastery. Meanwhile, the "brothers of the mountain," as the monks called them — that is, rebels opposing the military regime — visited the monastery, in particular Emir Saya Attyah and several armed men, on the evening of Christmas in 1993.

The monks at Atlas, unwavering in solidarity with their Muslim neighbors, refused to abandon the monastery even after authorities repeatedly insisted. Their discernment to stay in Tibhirine was the fruit of lengthy community meetings and advice from the archbishop of Algiers.

On January 2, 1994, the bishops of Algeria published "A Message to the Christians of Algeria," in which they declared:

Walking together with the Algerian people, we are overwhelmed by a whirlwind crisis and are still awaiting a solution. We do not know what the future holds. We must help one another make whatever daily offering is necessary. In the days and weeks to come, we will probably have to reflect together on the decisions we are obliged to make given certain events and situations. Everyone, with the help of his brothers and sisters, must be given the freedom to decide what is best.

Archbishop Teissier wrote a letter to priests, religious, and lay personnel in Algeria that clearly left open the possibility of death:

The greater the polarization and radicalization caused by recent events, the more meaningful our vocation appears. For a long time, we have offered our lives for this mission in response to the call we have received. We don't know ahead of time what road God will lead us down to live this offering to the end. ... We do not know the length of sacrifice required to fulfill our vocation.

Subsequently, the situation in Algeria deteriorated and ultimately broke down completely. On January 31, 1994, General Zeroual was appointed "President of State," but nothing was able to stop the escalating violence and terror. Numerous dissidents, imams, intellectuals, artists, journalists, doctors, lawyers, judges, and teachers were assassinated. Terrorists barricaded streets, planted car bombs, and abducted young girls as sex slaves. The military reacted in increasingly violent ways, even taking recourse to napalm to "extinguish clandestine resistance." Faced with this situation, foreign embassies evacuated most of their personnel.

Henri Teissier took inventory of the Church on March 25, 1994. He found that almost all foreign laity had fled. Only a small group of Christians was left, including local Algerians, African students, and some lay missionaries. Individual priests and entire communities were forced to leave their places of residence. The archbishop wrote, "We are not in Algeria to die as martyrs — that is, as victims at the hands of criminals. We are rather to live the Gospel of friendship with all our brothers and sisters without exception. ... If one suffers violence, the blow reaches every one of us."

In an editorial appearing in the diocesan newspaper of Orano, *Le Lien,* Pierre Claverie offered the following reflection:

> A Christian has a rightful place in an Islamic vision of society: he is respected insofar as he is the recipient of a preparatory revelation to Islam, and he is suspect insofar as he dares to not recognize the fullness of religion in Islam. Tolerated as dragging along a buried past on the way to reabsorption and Islamization, a Christian is suspected of conducting an ongoing crusade against Islam, an ongoing plot that assaults and attacks the Muslim fortress.

It was in this context that the first two murders of a religious man and woman were carried out in Algiers on, May 8, 1994. Nine more were killed by assassins' bullets before March 1996.

On the night of March 26-27, 1996, seven monks of the Atlas community — Christian, Luc, Christophe, Michel, Bruno, Célestin, and Paul — were abducted by an unknown local group, according to the testimony of a Muslim night watchman at the monastery. "Are there only seven of you?" one of the abductors asked the watchman, who responded with a vague nod, thus saving the lives of the other two brothers, Amédée and Jean-Pierre. Brother Bruno was captured immediately after his arrival, that very evening in Fez, Morocco, for the election of the prior, which was to take place a few days later. There were various people staying in the guesthouse that night who had come to participate in the meeting of *Ribat es Salam*.

On April 26, 1996, an absurd request was circulated by the GIA in London, asking French President Jacques Chirac to free Abdelhak Layada, who was being held in an Algerian jail. According to the second and last message from the unknown criminal group, the throats of the seven monks were slit on May 21. Their remains — consisting of no more than severed heads — were discovered May 25 at the gates of Medea. The Algerian government officially announced their murder on May 30. On the same day, ninety-two-year-old Cardinal Duval died of grief, "crucified" by the disappearance of the monks after he so ardently supported their silent presence in Algeria. The funeral of the former archbishop of Algiers and the seven monks was celebrated in the Basilica of Notre-Dame d'Afrique in Algiers on June 2, 1996. They were buried in Tibhirine on June 4, 1996.

Dom Olivera, abbot general of the Cistercians, would later say, "The seven coffins, each adorned with a red rose, were arranged in a large, sparsely decorated room. Contemplating in their presence, we could not help but think of Jesus' forerunner, John the Baptist," referring to the latter's death at the hands of Herod, who feared the threat John posed to his power.

A few Trappists volunteered to return to Algeria between 1998 and 2001, though they were unable to take up residence at Tibhirine for security reasons. The Monastery of Our Lady of Atlas was officially transferred to Midelt in Morocco in 1998. Brother Jean-Pierre, one of the survivors of the attack on the Tibhirine community, went to join them.

On May 21, 2001, the place then called Notre-Dame de Tibhirine was entrusted to the Diocese of Algiers, and, for about fifteen years, Father Jean-Marie Lassausse, a priest-agronomist, cared for the fruit trees and plants on the property. The community of *Chemin Neuf* took over the monastery in 2016. This Catholic community, composed of families and consecrated celibates, men and women, has roots in the Ignatian spiritual tradition and the ecumenical experience of the charismatic renewal. Several at the Tibhirine monastery are engaged in farming, beekeeping, and tending livestock in collaboration with residents of the village in the fraternal spirit of the martyrs of Atlas, based on friendship and prayer. The monastery accepts a growing number of pilgrims, mostly Muslims, who go there to pray, all with the same sentiments, at the tombs of these seven bright witnesses to invincible hope.

Brief Portraits of the Seven Blessed Martyrs

Brother Luc, physician, eighty-two years old

Born in 1914 at Bourg-le-Péage in the department of Drôme in southeastern France, Paul Dochier studied medicine at Lyon and performed military service in Morocco before returning to monastic life at the encouragement of the great French mystic Marthe Robin, who died in 1981. He entered the monastery in Aiguebelle (Drôme) in 1941. While voluntarily detained in place of a father with children, Dochier took special care of Russian prisoners suffering from typhus fever.

On August 28, 1946, on the feast of Saint Augustine, he arrived at Tibhirine, where he took on the management of the health clinic. He made his religious profession in 1949, asking to remain a simple lay brother rather than being ordained a priest. During the Algerian War of Independence (1954–1962) between France and the Algerian National Liberation Front, he was taken prisoner by the latter, but released a few days later. The care he gave to everyone indiscriminately was taken by the French army as an affront, and was later taken the same way by the Algerian army.

Respected by the local people, Dochier was considered a physician of both body and soul. Even though he suffered from asthma, he worked tirelessly, humbly, and with a healthy sense of humor. Everyone referred to him by his nickname "Frélou" (a contraction of "Fratel Luc"). During his imprisonment in 1996, in the last recording of his voice released by the French Embassy on April 30, he proved his internal freedom as he made a quip about the ironic name of his captors: "What do you call yourselves again?"

Father Bruno, former teacher, sixty-six years old
Christian Lemarchand was born in 1930 in the department of Deux-Sèvres in east-central France. Part of his family was Protestant. Because his father was an army official, Christian spent most of his infancy in Algeria in Orléansville (now Chlef, east of Algiers), where he received his first Communion and confirmation before his sister died there in 1938 at the age of sixteen.

During the Second World War, the "Cœurs Vaillants" (Courageous Hearts) and "Eucharistic Crusade" had a profound effect on Christian. A teacher, he was ordained to the priesthood in 1956 and attached himself to the "Charles de Foucauld" priestly fraternity. He frequently visited the Abbey of Bellefontaine (Maine-et-Loire in eastern France), which he officially entered in 1981 at the age of fifty-one, taking the name Bruno. He spent some months at Tibhirine in 1984 and then definitively joined in 1990, before becoming superior of the monastery at Fez in Morocco.

A few days before his abduction, Bruno came to Tibhirine to participate in the upcoming election of the new prior, which had been planned for March 31. He was abducted erroneously in the place of another member of Tibhirine on the night of March 26, 1996, together with six other brothers, including Célestin and Michel, who also came from the Abbey of Bellefontaine.

Brother Célestin, former "street teacher," sixty-two years old
Born in 1933 in Touvois in the department of Loire Atlantique, Célestin Ringeard had a difficult childhood following the premature death of his father. He, like Christian de Chergé and Paul Favre-Miville, served as a French soldier in the Algerian War, working in the army's medical unit. When a group of soldiers argued for the mercy killing of an official from the *Front de Libération Nationale* named Si Ahmed Hallouz, Célestin saved his life and created a bond of friendship with him. After returning to France in 1960 and being ordained a priest, he chose to become a street educator to help alcoholics, criminals, and prostitutes.

The priestly fraternity *Jesus Caritas*, inspired by the spirituality of Charles de Foucauld, was a great help to Célestin. Attracted to the monastic life, he entered the monastery at Bellefontaine in 1983 and then went to Tibhirine in 1986, following two other brothers of the same community, Brother Michel and Brother Bruno. A sign "even more marvelous than a miracle," he was immediately welcomed upon his arrival in Algeria by an ex-prisoner, Si Ahmed Hallouz, whom he had not seen for twenty-eight years. He professed his perpetual vows in Tibhirine on April 30, 1989, the feast of Our Lady of Africa. Of fragile health, he had to undergo several cardiac bypass surgeries, but his faithfulness to the monastery never wavered. He was entrusted with liturgical duties, serving as cantor for the community. "We are brothers of the Paschal Lamb!" he wrote in 1994, three months after an emir from the Armed Islamic Group visited the monastery.

Dom Christian de Chergé, prior, fifty-nine years old
Christian de Chergé was born in 1937 in Colmar, located in the

department of Haut-Rhin, in northeastern France, to a family of eight children. The Boy Scouts had an enormous impact on him. While he was serving as an SAS official (Specialized Administrative Section) in the French Army during the Algerian War, a Muslim field guard by the name of Mohammed gave his life for him by sparing him from *fellaghas* (armed militants). This was a key factor in his decision to return to Algeria to serve as an agent of peace between differing communities, dedicating himself to prayer and witness to universal brotherhood.

He entered the Abbey of Aiguebelle — the mother abbey of the Atlas community — in 1969. He subsequently left for Atlas in 1971, making his solemn religious profession in 1976. In 1979, he cofounded the group dedicated to fostering friendship between Muslims and Christians, *Ribat es Salam*. Elected prior in 1984 and reelected in 1990, he had a profound spiritual influence on Tibhirine and the numerous guests who visited the community, especially with his indomitable fidelity to the Algerian people. His *Testament*, dated December 1, 1993, on the anniversary of the death of Charles de Foucauld, is a masterpiece of contemporary religious literature (see appendix 1).

Brother Paul, former plumber, fifty-seven years old
Paul Favre-Miville, born in 1939 in Vinzier (department of Haute-Savoie) to a family of four children, began manual labor at a young age to help his father as a metalworker in the forge. He served in the airborne division during the Algerian War, achieving the rank of second lieutenant. Upon his return to France, he reentered the labor force, this time as a plumbing specialist. He dedicated himself to serving the community as a fire department volunteer. He also volunteered regularly with the *Cité Saint-Pierre du Secours Catholique* in Lourdes, serving the poorest pilgrims. He entered the Tamié Abbey (Savoie) in 1984 and arrived at Tibhirine in 1989, yearning to rediscover the country he had

fallen in love with at the age of twenty, just like the other monks who had participated in the Algerian War: Christian, Célestin, and Bruno. At Tibhirine, Brother Paul was responsible for the irrigation system, making sure the plants were well watered. He professed his solemn vows on August 20, 1991, affirming his desire to deepen his faith together with the other brothers of Atlas and maintain strong communal bonds with the people of the village by living a simple life of solidarity with them.

Brother Fleury, former manual laborer, fifty-two years old
Born in 1944 in western France, Michel Fleury helped his father in the workshop from an early age. After studying in the seminary for several years, he discerned that he would best serve as a laborer in the humble spirit of Blessed Father Antoine Chevrier, founder of the *Istituto del Prado*. He earned his industrial professional certification for mechanical parts manufacturing and entered the trade union, working first in Lyon, then Paris, and finally Marseilles, living for a time in community in a house that welcomed Muslim immigrants from the Maghreb. His attraction to a life of prayer led him initially to the Abbey of Bellefontaine in 1980, then to Tibhirine in 1984, where he met up with Brother Bruno and made his solemn profession on August 28, 1986. He was both the cook and gardener of the community.

"Holy Creator Spirit, join me to the Paschal Mystery of Jesus Christ, our Lord, as quickly as possible, by whatever means you deign fitting. Yet let not my will be done, but yours," Paul wrote as an act of offering on May 30, 1993. After the abduction of the seven monks, his monastic habit — the sign of his definitive commitment — was found along the side of a footpath, the last trace of a life offered as complete gift.

Father Christophe, minister to disabled children, forty-five years old

Christophe Lebreton was born in 1950 in Blois, in the center of France, to a family of twelve children. From his earliest student days, he dedicated himself to serving the most disadvantaged, especially by collaborating with the *Emmaus* community founded by Abbé Pierre. Ministering to disabled children in Algeria, Christophe discovered Tibhirine thanks to Father Joseph Carmona, then pastor of Hussein-Dey in Algiers. He entered the Tamié Abbey at a young age, making his religious profession in 1980. He subsequently received professional training as a carpenter. Sensing that the monastery at Tibhirine needed more help, he willingly left for Atlas in October 1987 and was ordained to the priesthood by Archbishop Teissier in 1990. His main responsibilities in the community were the liturgy and the agricultural cooperative together with some of the Muslim neighbors. A member of *Ribat es Salam* and full of love for God, his writings are marked by a strong poetic character and extraordinary spiritual depth. He was the youngest of the seven martyrs. As vice-prior and novice master, he may well have been elected prior on March 31, 1996, just as Brother Christian had wished.

Chapter 1

CALLED TO MAKE A GIFT OF SELF IN THE LITTLE THINGS OF THE EVERYDAY

E ach of us, no matter our state in life, is called to live in openness to our neighbor, to change our priorities in order to root
ourselves in the essential. This leads to a new way of ordering our
lives, a new way of loving that has its source in God's love, a new
way of carrying out our jobs as coworkers in building up God's
kingdom rather than seeking personal enrichment. We can make
ourselves a means for others to achieve holiness through the simplicity and balance of our lives as we humbly serve our brothers
and sisters. In the washing of the feet, Jesus teaches us to place
ourselves at the service of one another, humbly and with tenderness and love.

In 2013, during a diocesan pilgrimage to Tibhirine in the Year
of Faith, Paul Desfarges, then bishop of Constantine and Hippo

(a successor of Saint Augustine), quoted from a homily given by Father Christian de Chergé on Holy Thursday, in which the latter — the prior of Our Lady of Atlas — demonstrates the extent to which the vocation of every baptized Christian is a "martyrdom of love," simply meaning that we are to "give of ourselves in little things."

As violence was spreading across Algeria, even encroaching on the monastery, Brother Christian already had this to say to his brothers on March 31, 1994, two years before the abduction:

> Jesus' witness until death — his "martyrdom" — was a martyrdom of love: love for mankind, for each and every human person. A love that extends to thieves, assassins, and torturers, and all those living in darkness, ready to treat him and you as a sheep destined for slaughter (Ps 44:12). ... In Jesus' mind, friends and enemies are born of the same Father: you are all brothers! The fact is that martyrdom includes forgiveness. It is a perfect gift; the gift God makes without hesitation. Therefore, the washing of feet, the sharing of bread, and the handing of oneself over to death, and forgiveness — they are all one thing, and they are one for all ... it is where we find the greatest freedom, because to choose the Son means to choose the Father's love.

The prior of Tibhirine went on:

> To give our lives for the sake of God's love — ahead of time and without condition — this is what we have done, or at least this is what we believed we were doing. We didn't ask how or why then. We simply entrusted ourselves to God so that he could use us to carry out his plans day after day until the end.

After quoting Brother Christian's moving homily, Bishop Desfarges noted that the call to this martyrdom of love is the call of every baptized person, because "when we are baptized we are clothed with Christ, and our lives are caught up into the very life of Christ. ... Our daily witness must take the form of washing the feet of others — that is, to give ourselves in service."

Brother Christian also had this to say to his fellow monks on Holy Thursday:

> My goodness, we have all lived long enough to know it is impossible to do everything out of love and to pretend that every moment of our lives is a constant witness of love, a "martyrdom" of love. ... We know from experience that little gestures cost much, especially when we have to repeat them day after day. To wash our brother's feet is fine on Holy Thursday, but if we have to do it every day of the year as if we were doing it for the first time? That is a different story. ... We have given our hearts "wholly" to God, and it costs much to love him in every single detail of our lives. To put a towel around our waist like Jesus means nothing less than to give our entire lives. At the same time, to give our lives may mean something as simple as putting a towel around our waists.

Commenting on this homily, Bishop Desfarges, who was made archbishop of Algiers in 2016, emphasized the extent to which "this kind of witness inspires us to focus on the simple things in our daily lives: what we encounter in our families, our schools, our universities, our communities, our neighborhoods, and in our countless daily activities and responsibilities. ... Every human act, even the most humble, is enshrouded in an infinite, eternal mystery, when it is turned into an act of love." He invited the pilgrims to Tibhirine, past and future, to keep their gaze fixed on Mary: "She spent her life in Bethlehem and Nazareth giving witness with a towel wrapped around her waist, never making a fuss, but rather making herself transparent to the Presence of the One who comes to dwell among his own. Our Lady of Atlas, grant us the grace of a heart that loves and desires to love more and more each day."

The seven monks were rooted in the reality of the day-to-day. They showed this precisely in their solidarity of action, coming together with members of other religions, offering hospitality to strangers, sharing the joys and sorrows of their Muslim neighbors ... the examples go on and on. In this first chapter, we pay special attention to Brother Paul, whom the locals often encountered dressed in blue overalls at the wheel of the monastery car filled with tubes and supplies for the irrigation system in the community garden.

The residents of Medea, like those of Tibhirine, felt very close to the working monks. They looked up to Brother Paul and appreciated his care for the irrigation system which was essential for the farming of the community. Paul had great affection for his father, a metalworker in the Alpine region of Savoie, but his heart was in Algeria from the time he performed military service in the airborne division during the War of Independence. He was stationed in Blida, not far from Tibhirine.

Gifted with an open spirit and a wonderful sense of humor, Brother Paul always made himself available and was thoroughly social, making his entry into the Cistercian monastery at Tamié at the age of forty-five a big surprise for everyone who knew him. He was a normal, everyday sort of person, upstanding and faithful in his duties before becoming a monk. He was a volunteer firefighter, a member of the village choir, a member of the town council, a stretcher bearer at the shrine at Lourdes — he was a man who gave himself completely in heartfelt and humble prayer, transforming the everyday into an opportunity for grace. This is how he summoned everyone to a peaceful, joyful, serene, upbeat, brotherly life. His sense of humor was unforgettable. Speaking in a way that never failed to make everyone laugh was his special way of connecting with others. That was his way of avoiding the risk of hurting others. That was his way of expressing love. There is an old proverb that successful living in a monastery is 50 percent love and 50 percent good humor.

Father Christophe, one of the seven Atlas martyrs, preceded Brother Paul in the abbey that Christian de Chergé came to in search of vocations. This instilled in Brother Paul a desire to leave for Algeria in 1989 after the death of his father. It was his heart's desire to maintain the Christian presence in Algeria so that it could witness to the reality of Christ's body through a life of simplicity.

"The Spirit is alive, working in the depths of the human heart. Let us strive to keep ourselves open so that He might work in us through prayer and enkindle in us a love for all our brothers," he wrote in a letter dated January 1995 during the darkest days of the civil war. "What will be left of the Church in Algeria in a few months? What will become of its witness, its structures, its people? Perhaps very little, if anything. Yet I am still convinced that the Good News has been planted and that the seed is germinating," he wrote in the same letter. What really mattered in his eyes — in the words of Pope Francis's *Gaudete et Exsultate* — was "to live the present moment, filling it to the brim with love" (17).

By living and loving in the present moment, the monks of Tibhirine, "simply Christians," united themselves to the "today" of God.

As the factotum of the priory, Brother Paul took special care of the workshop and the heating of the old building as he helped Father Christophe in the garden along with some Algerian neighbors. Brother Jean-Pierre — who survived the tragedy — was fond of recalling how Brother Paul always had his hands full of "grease, oil, motors, and cables, yet he was never absent from liturgy, and he always looked serene and organized."

The daily collaboration between "Brother Factotum," Father Christophe, and local residents, the continual care of the sick due to Brother Luc's dedication to the health clinic, the cordiality of gatekeeper Brother Amédée, Jean-Pierre's shopping runs to the city, the warm welcome offered to guests by guest master Brother Michel, who also worked in the kitchen — everything was lived in a spirit of service, fidelity, abandonment, and humility.

This community — "silent, simple, and authentic," as described by Father Christophe — was composed of "men who dared — humbly and peacefully — to witness to the fact that it is well worth giving your life to God in community through prayer, adoration, and living the Beatitudes … and in this way to learn how to love, and to love until each day is finally over."

"To love until each day is finally over" in a profound coherence between the ideal life and our concrete, everyday living — that is, the daily grind — characterizes the message the brothers of Atlas strove to give, in that their primary concern was to be authentic Trappist monks. The martyrdom simply followed upon this.

Nevertheless, "this does not pertain to monks and nuns alone: we are all called to give our lives in the details of the everyday, in our families, at work, in our communities, in service to our 'common home' and to the good of all," Pope Francis clearly affirmed in his preface to a collected volume entitled *Tibhirine, l'eredità*. "Twenty years after their death," he continues, "we, in turn, are invited to be signs of simplicity and mercy in the daily exercise of giving ourselves after the example of Christ."

In the same spirit of Tibhirine, the Holy Father develops the appeal he makes in *Gaudete et Exsultate*, recalling how Jesus invited his disciples to pay attention to details:

The little detail that wine was running out at a party. The

little detail that one sheep was missing. The little detail of noticing the widow who offered her two small coins. The little detail of having spare oil for the lamps, should the bridegroom delay. The little detail of asking the disciples how many loaves of bread they had. The little detail of having a fire burning and a fish cooking as he waited for the disciples at daybreak. A community that cherishes the little details of love, whose members care for one another and create an open and evangelizing environment, is a place where the risen Lord is present, sanctifying it in accordance with the Father's plan. (144–145)

Chapter 2

PRAYING TOGETHER, IN THE CHURCH

P raying is an essential act of faith in God's grace: Prayer never starts with us. It begins with God, who invites us to prayer. Consequently, prayer places us in a right relationship with God. It opens our spirit. Without this opening, we lose our balance. Prayer is not an activity reserved for monks and nuns. It is not even exclusive to Christians. There is, however, something specific to Christian prayer: to keep the prayer of Jesus himself alive. Christian prayer "proclaims" Jesus in this way.

There is a twofold witness to monastic life: The spiritual battle of Jesus for the salvation of the world occurs through the monk's sprayer, and his intercession builds a bridge between the interiority of his relationship with God and his solidarity with all human beings. When, through prayer, a Christian (or a Christian community) is united with Christ, he enters into the work of the Savior "for the glory of God and the salvation of the world."[1]

"The beautiful scent has spread throughout the world, the cut flower rests on the land of Algeria," said a brother of *Chemin Neuf* — the community that took the place of the Tibhirine monks in 2016 — emphasizing, in a meditative way, our common mission to get to the "praying roots" of the martyrs of Atlas.

Giving witness to a praying Church was, after all, the foremost reason the Cistercian monks were called to Algeria. "Christians don't pray. They act like dogs," complained the Algerian Muslims, beginning with Emir Abdelkader, leader of the Algerian resistance during the French colonial invasion. Abdelkader was a spiritual guide, a gentleman, and a knight who preached by example, treating prisoners of war with utmost sympathy.

His comment about the lack of prayer of Christians and his comparison of them to animals made an impression on his opponent, General Bugeaud, the leader of the colonial army, who was the one to suggest the establishment of a contemplative monastery in the land. The bishop of Algiers, Antoine-Louis-Adolphe Dupuch, who later became close friends with the emir after the latter was taken prisoner, asked the Trappists to establish a monastery near Algiers. As we have seen, this is the origin of the village referred to as La Trappa since 1843.

To show how ardently they wanted to build a bridge between the two religious confessions, the monks commissioned a magnificent statue of Mary the Mother of Jesus — a title beloved by Muslims, seeing as she is the only woman that the Koran refers to by name. On the highest part of the property, the statue, made in Toulouse and initially enshrined at the Cistercian settlement in Staouéli, became a "sign on the mountain" as she kept vigil over the local population and the Cistercian monks.

Although she has lost her arms and her face is marred, the old statue still stands at Tibhirine on the hilltop of Abdelkader. There is discussion on whether she should be restored because the inhabitants of the village are very fond of her, faithful to the memory of the monks who visited her frequently to beg God's help at her feet. "Mary is the guarantee of total and radical detachment for God,"[2] wrote Father Christophe in January 1994, reflecting on her vocation to fruitful chastity: "I do not belong to myself."

In 1972, the basement of the property, which had once been a wine cellar, became the monastery chapel. The brothers had resolved to live in closer communion with their Muslim neighbors. Every Wednesday, at the time of the Eucharist, which was also the most important hour for Muslim prayer, placing together in the same act of praise all their acts of love, the renouncement of themselves, and their charitable sacrifices, they united themselves to the blood of Christ poured out to reconcile mankind to God. "Praying among others who pray," according to the expression used by the brothers of Atlas from 1975, the monks contributed to making the Catholic Church respectable and credible in the eyes of Islamic believers. Among other things, Cardinal Duval once remarked to the monks that their daily routine as men dedicated to prayer was the best way to help Muslims understand the Church's attitude toward Islam. "We could even say that a lack of this kind of witness seriously harms the Church and thwarts Islam-Christian dialogue,"[3] the prior of Atlas said in 1995, one year before his death, well aware of the imminent danger. He explained that as "praying men among people of prayer," their vocation was an *opus Dei*, a work of God, building up communion to overcome boundaries. Their neighbors sensed the depth of this spiritual life. When he was a soldier during the Algerian War, Father Christian stipulated a "prayer contract" with a Muslim friend. This friend, a member of the military scouting contingent whose name was Muhammed, was killed while trying to protect Christian in a shootout after saying to him: "I know that you will pray for me ... but, you see, Christians don't know how to pray!" This encounter helped plant the seed of a monastic vocation in

Christian, who looked forward to the opportunity to pray in communion in an Islamic land. The prior was fond of citing a passage of Max Thurian di Taizé, as he did during a Lenten service on March 8, 1996: "It is important that the Church ensure a fraternal presence of men and women who live communally with Muslims in silence, prayer, and friendship."[4]

As Pope Francis recalled in his apostolic constitution *Vultum Dei Quaerere*, liturgical and personal prayer is a fundamental necessity for nourishing the entire contemplative life: "If prayer is the 'core' of consecrated life, it is even more so for the contemplative life" (16). There are many people today who do not know how to pray. Indeed, many feel no need to pray, or they pray to God only in moments of serious difficulty when they don't know to whom they can turn. Others reduce prayer to an act of praise in moments of joy. Contemplatives become the voice for these people and intercede for the salvation of all mankind, just as the prophets did.

In fact, if communal and personal prayer is essential for Cistercians, the prayerful reading of Scripture is just as important, as Father Christian wrote to the monks while Algeria was being torn asunder by war: "Pick up the Book at night, while others are picking up arms."[5] More than thirty years after Algeria's independence, in a Muslim country tragically pierced by hate, the only bell still ringing was that of Tibhirine, signaling lauds, matins, terce, sext, none, vespers, and compline.

The spirit of Assisi that was born out of the meeting of world religions organized by Saint John Paul II in 1986 left a lasting mark on the community. In fact, the brothers were convinced that the various religions could and should contribute to peace and teach a respect for conscience, love of neighbor, forgiveness, prayer, and so on. It was this spirit that prompted the monks to make a prayer room available to Muslims, who are called to pray five times a day. "The monastery bells and the muezzin rang out in succession from the same, enclosed space, making it difficult to ignore the call to prayer from both sources, as if it were recalling everyone to the communion that filled the heart of Him to whom we all turn with the same abandonment,"[6] Father Christian said in a talk he gave in Rome in 1989 at the Pontifical Institute for Arab and Islamic Studies. It is an invitation for us Christians to come out of ourselves, because peace, by its very nature, is universal and transcends the boundaries of race and religion.

The fraternal presence of the monks fostered an openness to accept God's creative power, gradually bridging these two communities — Christian and Muslim — in a dynamic communion, as Father Christian expressed at a gathering of priests:

> It is precisely prayer that allows me to assign each of the brothers the task appropriate for him, besides encouraging him to get along with the other brothers. Furthermore, it allows me to perceive more clearly the similarities between them and not worry too much about the differences. The unity of all people in the Heart of Christ is more evident if we listen honestly and prayerfully to others. Then we will discover that the simpler the gestures and words we use to talk about spirituality, the easier it will be to overlook religious division. There are ways of speaking "religiously" in a universal way.[7]

This kind of speaking involves a "common emptying of desires to enkindle a more ardent desire for God," Father Christian added, explaining that if "we don't know how to pray as we ought ... the Spirit — and the Spirit alone — knows how to pray within us in an ineffable way ... the Spirit is the fire, and without him we grow cold. ... Moreover, when I resolve to offer Him nothing but my silence, I always know that something is really happening; that I am joining a symphony," he said with conviction, recalling that this "house of prayer," the temple of the Spirit that we are, is called to be truly "a house of prayer for all people," just as the prophet Isaiah said in chapter 56 in reference to the Temple of Jerusalem. In this way, the future martyrs became a means of "channeling the cries of others." They desired to pour themselves out constantly as a way of offering this universal prayer.

Praise, supplication, and intercession fostered an "atmosphere of humility," Father Christian said in a talk to the Little Sisters of Jesus, emphasizing that an acknowledgment of our "powerlessness" is necessary to "become docile to the Holy Spirit in prayer"[8] from moment to moment, and, just like Jesus, to open ourselves to the Father's will.

The Psalms and *lectio divina* — the prayer through which we ruminate on the Scriptures and receive nourishment from them — as well as the Eucharist, teach us to recognize that God is present in the ordinary events of our everyday lives. Inspired by this teaching and the living example of the brothers at Tibhirine, many laypeople throughout Algeria, after visiting the monastery, adopted the practice of praying the Liturgy of the Hours — a prayer not only for priests and deacons, but for everyone.

As a final call to prayer and an ultimate sign of the life the monks left behind, the locals preserved Brother Michel's "hood": the white habit he wore during the common recitation of the Divine Office, a symbol of his consecration and the offering of his daily life. It was found in the dewy grass along the street near the monastery on the morning of March 27, 1996, a few days after his abduction. Brother Michel's liturgical garment is a reminder of the "celebration" the seven monks of Atlas were called to, especially between the Ascension and Pentecost, in their perpetual bond to Christ's paschal mystery.

Brother Michel's witness, to which we now turn, is particularly enlightening. Because the prior saw in him a spirit of prayer and an ability to listen to the word of God in ways that were Marian, monastic, and Cistercian — something he had acquired in solidarity with other manual laborers through the *Istituto del Prado* — Brother Michel received the ministry of lector. Working side by side with the Moroccan laborers in France for many years and sharing their poverty, Brother Michel strove to live the Gospel without compromise and found in Tibhirine a way to unite the two aspects of his vocation: the spiritual life, and the life of an ongoing dialogue with Muslims.

"Holy Creator Spirit, join me to the Paschal Mystery of Jesus Christ, our Lord, as quickly as possible, by whatever means you deign fitting. Yet let not my will but yours be done,"[9] Brother Michel begged in his "act of self-giving" signed May 30, 1993, on the Feast of Pentecost, the Vigil of the Visitation and Eid al-Adha (Festival of the Sacrifice), a Muslim feast that commemorates the sacrifice of Abraham. His testament, written in pencil, was found by chance folded up in the pages of a book shelved away in the monastery's library.

Brother Michel's birthday was May 21, the presumed death date of the seven martyred monks, according to the statement of the GIA about the massacre. As Brother Michel wrote in a letter in December 1995: "May the blood of men of peace become a seed of peace!"[10]

In effect, the criminal operation that tried to build a wall between Christians and Muslims by framing global conflict as a "clash of civilizations" ended up strengthening interreligious dialogue and the fraternal bond between Muslims and Christians. This incredible miracle was undoubtedly the fruit of a life of prayer and intercession, a hidden spring within the monks' experience of solidarity and the way their message quietly spread throughout the world.

The great men and women of God were great intercessors. Intercession is like the "yeast" of the Trinity. It is the act of joining ourselves to the Father to discover the ways he enlightens concrete situations in our lives and empowers us to change them. The heart of God is moved by intercessory prayer, but the reality is that he always anticipates us, and what we really accomplish by interceding is to make his power, his love, and his fidelity more manifest to others.[11]

Chapter 3

WORKING IN THE FRUITFUL
SILENCE OF NAZARETH

Work, especially manual work, gives monks the opportunity to participate in God's creative-redemptive work and to walk in the footsteps of Jesus Christ. This principle has had a special place in the Cistercian tradition. In addition to being redemptive, manual work procures the brothers' everyday needs and the needs of others, especially the poor. It also manifests the monks' solidarity with millions of manual workers. It serves as an opportunity for asceticism, fostering personal development and maturation and keeping the body and spirit healthy. Finally, manual work makes a significant contribution to the cohesion of the entire community. This is how the Trappist Constitution presents work, as if it is the privileged means by which monks stay grounded.

The name of the settlement, written "Tib-Harine" during French colonization, was changed to "Tibhirine" after Algeria won independence in 1962. This name — which, to be precise, is pronounced "Tib-EH-irin" — means "watered garden" in the local Amazigh language — that is, the language of the Berbers. Atlas, at an altitude of three thousand feet, is blessed with abundant water, making it an ideal habitat for thriving, productive fruit trees.

Since gardening and farming offer wonderful opportunities to praise God, Trappists have worked this land for four to six hours a day since 1938. Saint Benedict, the father of Western monasticism, teaches that monks, "when they live and work with their hands, most resemble our forefathers and the apostles."[12]

When the monastery was transformed into a "Cistercian relic in an ocean of Islam," as Father Christian put it, the religious members of Our Lady of Atlas continued to farm the seventeen-acre plot, especially under the direction of Brother Christophe, the youngest of the group. The honey was also used to treat the sick in the medical clinic. The vegetables — tomatoes, beans, zucchini, etc. — were sold at market, just as fruit from hundreds of trees and the jams made from figs, plums, and cherries. Co-operative farming at Tibhirine, between the monks and their Muslim neighbors, became a basic way for the monks to implant themselves in the community. "We spoke with Mohammed about manuring and plowing this afternoon. ... This is a holy place. It is a place of true adoration in the spirit of Nazareth,"[13] Brother Christophe wrote in his diary in January 1994. One day in July 1994, before lauds, Mohammed asked Brother Christophe to borrow some hoes to dig up potatoes. He commented, "You know, it's like the same blood runs through us and keeps us going." "In this way," Christophe commented, "for him, blood speaks most of all of LIFE — given life, shared life."[14]

In caring for the garden and the liturgy, Brother Christophe took Saint Joseph — a Nazarene carpenter — as his model. Christophe jotted down a quote from Thomas Merton into his journal that says everything about his vocation as a silent worker: "My monastery … is a place in which I disappear from the world as an object of interest in order to be everywhere in it by hiddenness and compassion. In order to exist everywhere I had to become a no-one."

In the garden, by listening attentively to those striving to build a bridge between the two communities, fraternal bonds were forged between the monks and Ali, Moussa, Youssef, Mohammed, and Salim. Simple conversations took place every day between these Christians and Muslims around the topic of work. Some, like "Ammi Ali" (Uncle Ali), were truly the kind of wise old men whom Saint Benedict invited the novices to shower with honors.

In short, working the land was a special way for the monks to live socially and build friendships with their Muslim neighbors. "We had a sense that we were 'better understood' than other, older Christian monasteries in the area,"[15] the monks wrote in 1994 in a memo prepared for the Synod of Bishops on Consecrated Life.

"Living the repetitive cycle of Nazareth, without making a fuss, without doing anything really of note,"[16] the prior explained, noting that when God wishes to reveal himself through the words of Jesus Christ, this is precisely what he tells us in the parables, "and it was precisely among those workers that Jesus would seek his apostles."

"We are involved in ordinary work that has a quasi-sacramental value. This is precisely how we unite ourselves to the work of creation — by giving birth to something new each day — and to the work of redemption and suffering … as Saint Paul teaches," Father Christian profoundly remarked.

"In our order, work is done in the most ordinary way," he insisted, pointing out the tasks of cooking, gatekeeping, and hosting, not to mention keeping chickens. In reference to the communal experience, he added:

"The most mundane daily tasks are dignified whenever
we take to heart the need to do them with greater dedication ... attention to the smallest details can make our
love more vigilant in every moment of the day."

Nevertheless, the Rule of Saint Benedict governing the monks invites them to prefer nothing to the *opus Dei* ("the work of God"):
prayer. Work and prayer are not incompatible if we face life as
an integral whole that includes prayer, reading, manual activities,
and mutual service. Our manual and professional activities need
not be carried out in a utilitarian fashion or merely for the sake
of profit. When we join manual work to *lectio,* the liturgy, and
prayer, we can be transformed to the core. We have more direct
access to Jesus and his paschal mystery in our earthly state. It is a
way of life open to everyone.

Father Bruno expresses this beautifully in a prayer he composed: "Lead me, Lord, in silence and in prayer, in work and in
joyful service to my brothers after the example of your hidden life
in Nazareth."[17] His prayer touches upon the simplicity that is cen-
tral to the Cistercian tradition: a walk of discipline and wisdom
that can carry anyone to what is most essential through the grace
of shedding whatever is unnecessary and abandoning ourselves
to God so that we may be interiorly free and open to his will.
Announcing the kingdom through a simple life (*simplex*: that is,
"without wrinkles") — this was the meaning of the monks' lives.

In the simplicity of a daily life no different than ours, the
brothers of Atlas lived by the work of their hands, in the carpen-
try school of Nazareth, in the contemplation of the mystery of the
Incarnation. "Our forefathers in Cîteaux, and particularly Saint
Bernard, lovingly bent over the cradle of the Child Jesus, untir-
ingly contemplating the marvel of God's presence in such a new
and unprecedented way; a way so pervasive that His light did not
fail to penetrate every corner of human existence,"[18] the prior of

Tibhirine said to the community during a chapter meeting in December 1995. Father Christian de Chergé believed that Charles de Foucauld had a taste of the true "spirituality of Nazareth" in his monastic experience among the Trappists. In his spiritual testimony of December 1 — the anniversary of Charles de Foucauld's assassination in the remotest part of Algeria after being dragged from his hermitage in 1916 — Father Christian wrote:

> I reached a point where I had to ask myself whether Brother Alberic's[19] entrance into our order had some influence on his subsequent devotion to Jesus' hidden life in Nazareth. Was it by joining us — i.e., by taking on a "life of self-denial" dramatically different from his past — that he was able to discover such a hidden life? ... Or did he discover this "singular model" later — more specifically, in Nazareth — in a way the Trappist monastery was unable to give him?

Brother Alberic — who became brother Charles, the "universal brother" — was beatified on November 13, 2005, the year in which the cause for beatification of the nineteen Algerian martyrs, including the seven monks of Tibhirine, was opened. With eighty years of hindsight, it is abundantly clear that their witness is mysteriously connected to their love for the Algerian people.

The Little Sisters of Jesus, born out of Charles de Foucauld's inspiration to live the simple life of Nazareth among the poor, were very close to the monastery. In fact, Father Christophe gave retreats to the novices on several occasions. Strengthened by their habit of "visiting" the "school of Nazareth," the sisters helped Father Christophe to deepen his appreciation for the mystery of the Incarnation: the mystery of a birth that continued to the foot of the cross at Calvary. "Mary gives birth at the foot of the cross. It is time to be reborn: to come to the Eternal One who never ceases

saying, 'I love you.'"[20] Brother Christophe knew from experience
that the tops of trees do not point downward and that all creation
aspires to the things above. We will take a look at his inspirational
journey now. Together with his brothers, he kept his feet planted firmly on the ground, nourishing his hope in the "topsoil" of
small acts of charity performed throughout the day, never losing
sight of the "heavens" promised by the wood of the cross, the tree
of life whose fruits are offered to us every Easter morning, "the
victorious wounded lamb," the Risen Christ himself.

After having abandoned all religious practice in the tidal
wave of enthusiasm that swelled in May 1968, Christophe discovered Father de Foucauld. His writings kindled within him
a foolish desire to follow Jesus. At that time, he considered the
Little Brothers of Jesus and the spirituality of Brother Charles
before departing for Algeria for military service as an assistant
in a center for deaf, blind, and disabled children. He returned to
Our Lady of Atlas on several occasions and gradually heard an
interior call to become a Cistercian monk — a Trappist. In an
act of oblation dated August 15, 1982, he asked Mary, present on
Calvary, to grant him the "strength to imitate her son."[21] He went
to Tibhirine in 1987, an experience that gave him the strength
to remain steadfast in his friendship with his Muslim neighbors,
those for whom blood meant life. More importantly, he shared in
their communal life. "The battle of brother Luc: the praying doctor. May each of us do what he was called to do: to be in the workshop, kitchen, garden, or wherever as praying workers,"[22] Brother
Christophe observed. As a note in a symphony, work is impressed
upon the life of a monk as a continuation of liturgical and personal prayer; or rather, it strives to be prayer, a "prayer of the hands."
We, in turn, are called to remember that work is another way of
expressing our gift of self to God: We go to God not only with our
spirits, but also with our bodies.

In the last entry of Father Christophe's diary, dated March

19, 1996, the feast of Saint Joseph, he recalls an encounter with one of his Muslim neighbors. They were discussing marriage, just on the eve of his own call to the wedding feast of the Lamb and participation in the redemptive sacrifice that gave new birth to humanity:

> Today, on the anniversary of my consecration to Mary: Yes, I continue to choose you, Mary, with Joseph, in communion with all the saints. I receive you from the hands of Jesus with the poor and with sinners. Along with the Beloved Disciple, I take you into my home. Along with you, I am an offering. In the garden this morning I had a wonderful conversation with Moussa about marriage. I was blessed to preside at the Eucharist. I heard the voice of Joseph inviting me to sing Psalm 100 [101] with him and the Child Jesus: "I sing of mercy and justice. ... I study the way of integrity; when will you come to me? ... I walk with integrity of heart."[23]

This was the contribution of the "extroverted" Algerian Church, witnessing with the outpouring of its blood in a pluralistic and global age; the Church not as an end in herself, as if she were a little chapel reserved for her own members. As a whole, Christians have the specific vocation of building evangelical relationships with people of different beliefs. As Cardinal Duval put it, "I am convinced that fraternal love is the epiphany of the Christian message. It is through that message that the truth of the Gospel is revealed."[24]

> Sometimes it seems that our work is fruitless, but mission is not like a business transaction or investment, or even a humanitarian activity. It is not a show where we count how many people come as a result of our publici-

ty; it is something much deeper, which escapes all mea-
surement. It may be that the Lord uses our sacrifices to
shower blessings in another part of the world which we
will never visit. ... Let us learn to rest in the tenderness
of the arms of the Father amid our creative and generous
commitment. Let us keep marching forward; let us give
him everything, allowing him to make our efforts bear
fruit in his good time.[25]

Chapter 4

OVERCOMING A CHAIN
OF CRISES THROUGH A
SERIES OF REBIRTHS

Calling us to be builders of peace internally and externally, Jesus accompanies us on our personal, interior journey. He helps us to let go of whatever is passing and to accept whatever is to come. This is the genuine path to human maturity and a life more intensely focused on participating in the transformation of the world, each of us with his or her own abilities and duties.

When the electoral process in Algeria broke down after the Islamic Salvation Front was elected in January 1992, two armed groups formed in the country to fight against the "*junta*." They had their sights set on police agents and key political figures. As the months wore on, so did the car bombings, murders, violent explosions, and terrible retaliations. They were everyday occurrences. In the winter of 1995, Father Christophe wrote:

We had another meeting in Tibhirine yesterday ... workers, farmers, and our associates. It was beautiful and moving. Everybody expressed a desire to forge ahead. We witnessed a true resistance to the murderous violence that not only kills, but divides and instills a sense of desperation and insecurity into the populace. It is hard work to be a builder of peace, but it is also an immense joy.[26]

Within this active will for nonviolence, in the same year, in a chapter meeting in his community, Father Christian cited the wise words of Saint Jane Frances de Chantal: "Love is as foolish as death, and martyrs of love will suffer a thousand times more by preserving their lives to do the will of God than if they had to give it a thousand times to witness their faith, their love, and their fidelity."[27]

Encountering faceless barbarism in the country, the brothers of Atlas, more than ever, wanted to "stay together" — *cum-stare* — as the city of God where "everybody together *makes up the body*." "We are all tied — by mutual consensus — to the happiness of peace that the small population around us never ceases to hope for. The entire country continues to give us space, refusing to see themselves as living in an Algeria that drives out foreigners and brings non-Muslims to trial," the prior emphasized in a talk to his brothers.[28]

At another chapter meeting, Father Christian offered the example of the first desert father, Saint Anthony, who from the beginning of Christian monasticism decided to "lose his life," not by shedding his blood and giving himself over to the hate of the pagans, but rather through a "drop by drop" martyrdom, giving witness to the Gospel, listening and living according to the word of God, living it in every detail in the present moment. The future martyrs of Tibhirine once more saw in this choice "the specific fruitfulness" of their consecrated life.

The most acute phase of the crisis began when the GIA (Armed Islamic Group) issued an ultimatum in October 1993 that all foreigners leave Algerian territory within three months. Once the time expired, citizens of foreign countries were sought and killed: a Spaniard, a Frenchman, a Russian, a British national … then it was the ex-Yugoslavians, assassinated in the plumbers' borough of Tamesguida, about two and a half miles from the monastery, probably chosen due to the conflict in Bosnia. This was a shock to the Tibhirine community, because they knew the victims well. They were Christian Croats who came to pray with the monks at Christmas and Easter.

Around 7:15 p.m. on December 24, 1993, six mujahideen, wearing turbans in the Afghan style, burst into the monastery. Among them was emir Saya Attyah, who had ordered the Croats' execution. They explained that they were trying to distinguish between the "foreigners" and the "Christians," and they were waiting for the monks to help, "because they had helped their brothers during the first revolution with medical and material assistance."[29] The emir promised the Cistercian monks *aman* — a kind of protection — if they in return received medical assistance from them. Brother Luc was asked to go to the mountains to care for wounded rebels. Mindful of the advanced age of the doctor-brother, Father Christian denied the request, making an exception "for the injured who are well enough to come to the monastery," said Brother Jean-Pierre, one of the two who survived the Tibhirine massacre.[30]

The prior explained to the man in Arabic that the monastic community was preparing for the "feast of the birth of the Prince of Peace" that evening. The members of the armed group then excused themselves and left, adding that they would return using the code name "Lord Christian."

Subsequently, word came back that the leader of the Islamic group — only miles from the monastery — was agonizing for nine days, refusing to ask for Brother Luc, the elderly doctor, to come to him because he had accepted the terms imposed by the prior in negotiations with the monastery. "Every crime of his is horrible, but he is not a dirty beast,"[31] Father Christian said later in Algiers.

In such extreme conditions, feeling pressure from the Algerian authorities insisting that the monks leave the monastery for the "official" reason that this was the only way to avoid their "collective suicide," the decision to remain was not easy. The Trappist monks tried with all their might to put into practice the advice they had received from the elderly Cardinal Duval after an Islamic group first barged into their monastery on Christmas Day in 1993: "steadfastness."

In monastic life, this steadfastness is expressed in a monk's vow to live stably in a fixed place. He ties himself to a specific community. In effect, the Rule of Saint Benedict defines the monastery as a workshop in which a monk must work diligently throughout his entire life. In a world where physical and technological mobility has become a lifestyle, the monastic way offers a radical alternative: One can remain in the same place, in the same community, and stay "fixed" on God.

Such stability may be interpreted more generally as the capacity to endure, and this is something that pertains to each and every one of us. All of us are able to embrace the "vow" in this sense. Committed to following Christ in whatever vocation we have received, we are called to fidelity and perseverance. There are different vocational journeys that root us in the stability of Christ's love. The way of the brothers at Tibhirine is but one.

So, the abrupt visit of the GIA opened up a multitude of possibilities to the brothers, and perhaps if we had been in their shoes, we might have chosen to flee immediately. Yet the monks did the opposite, responding in a way that could only be described as inspired from above.

"After the militants left, all we could do was carry on with our lives. We celebrated midnight Mass ... we sang traditional Christmas hymns and welcomed the Child Jesus, who came to us vulnerable and at risk. In fact, the 'massacre of the innocents' — that is, the Croats — occurred right before Christmas," Father Christian explained.[32]

"At that time," he said, "the ability to carry on with the rhythm of daily tasks was our salvation: the kitchen, the garden, the workshop, the land ... day after day.

"We had to disarm ourselves and renounce all violence, which would have amounted to nothing but an escalation of provocation and counter-provocation," he added, encouraging his brothers — and their friends — to look at things in this way to discover that "what Jesus invites us to do is to be reborn."

Jesus Christ is never finished being born within us. He wants to be born yet again in the hearts and minds of men and women today. He knocks at the door of our hearts, asking to be born there spiritually.

"Our identity as human beings is passed on from birth to birth, leading from one beginning to the next ... and from birth to birth, we will present the Son of God within us; because the Incarnation consists in allowing Jesus' sonship to be incarnated in our humanity, in *my* humanity ... the Church is the on-going incarnation ... from day to day, it relies on us alone ... for better or worse."[33]

Notwithstanding the risk and sense of anxiety, and immersed in the thick of the crisis, the monks found their true interior motivation to remain at Tibhirine for the feast of the Incarnation.

In threefold fidelity — to their ecclesial mission, to their monastic call, and to the Algerian people — the Trappists of Tibhirine refused to leave because they obtained true "freedom in the Spirit." Father Christophe testified to this in his diary:

We would make ourselves accomplices if we do not dis-
obey (vehemently!) the request made by phone. ... I rather have something else in mind: to become accomplices
of the Innocent One. To receive from Him our attitudes,
gestures, and words — adapted precisely to the measure
of our listening, our availability, our obedience. I am lean-
ing on the freedom of the spirit. He is our DEFENDER.[34]

Refusing to take sides in any way, their freedom became stronger
and stronger through various crises, during which they experi-
enced things beautifully expressed in *The Book of Faith,* written
by the bishops of the Maghreb and primarily by Dominican Father Pierre Claverie, bishop of Orano, who also died a martyr:

"In fidelity to Christ who chose the way of a Servant to
live out the encounter, the Christian knows he is called
to find, in his weakness, an opportunity to accept God's
strength."[35]

Precisely because we are weak, the Lord's grace can work within
us. That is the heart of the Gospel and the heart of the life of those
who follow Jesus. We are Christians, baptized into a life of following Christ, but we always find it difficult to advance according to
Christ's logic until the day we receive grace. This is the intuition
that had already matured within the silent heart of Christian de
Chergé during a personal crisis in 1979, three years before his
perpetual vows at Our Lady of Atlas, when he took a few months'
retreat at Assekrem in the remotest part of the Algerian desert at
the hermitage of Father de Foucauld. His testament, definitively
signed on the anniversary of Blessed Charles de Foucauld's death
(December 1, 1994), provides the hermeneutical key to the pilgrimage of nonviolence that ultimately cost the lives of the sev-
en martyrs of Tibhirine: "I would like it if my community, my

Church, my family, remember that my life was GIVEN to God and to this country."[36]

Each of the seven monks made his own free choice after his sojourn in the desert. In this chapter, we take a special look at Father Célestin, the cantor and ex-teacher of street kids who dedicated himself to serving victims of prostitution and alcohol abuse.

Having a somewhat exasperated disposition, Célestin knew his limitations and weaknesses, but he transformed them into a way of life. We must start precisely where we really are if we want to make progress in our spiritual lives. With Célestin, we are invited to embrace our own reality — that is, "to become a child once again." We know that God accepts us precisely as we are, and he comes to meet us precisely where we are.

Father Célestin was deeply afflicted by physical suffering. He had to undergo six emergency bypass surgeries in France after the events of Christmas 1993, which had knocked him out emotionally and physically. Still with a weak heart, he returned to Tibhirine as soon as he could, in September 1994, strengthened by that "infinite love of God who imprints the names of us little ones on the palms of his giant hands."[37] He added a prophetic note: "We are brothers of the Paschal Lamb!"

Father Célestin advocated nonviolence for a long time. During the Algerian War, he saved the life of a soldier in the National Liberation Army named Si Ahmed Hallouz, whom he ran into again after having become a monk at Atlas in 1986, a time he referred to as a "rebirth." How could he ever imagine that ten years later he would be abducted and killed by Algerians?

Overloaded and exhausted, he and his brother monks heard of the assassinations of Sister Paul-Hélène and Brother Henri Vergès, of the religious women Esther and Caridad, of the four White Fathers of Cabilia — Jean, Alain, Charles, and Christian — and of the religious women Angèle-Marie and Bibiane, and of Sister Odette.

Even as the tide of violence against religious men and women was on the rise, the Trappist community never stopped loving the people around them, drawing inspiration from the Book of Revelation. "Yes, this is all about you, the Victorious Lamb who was slain. This is all about you. I only hope to be swept up in the tide of the LIFE that has been given,"[38] Brother Christophe wrote in his diary on behalf of the whole community.

By this time, the Spirit of Christ was their interior law, the Holy Spirit given to men so that they might become facilitators of universal reconciliation and cooperators in God's new creation with their fellow men.

As Pope Francis wrote:

Every period of history is marked by the presence of human weakness, self-absorption, complacency and selfishness, to say nothing of the concupiscence which preys upon us all. These things are ever present under one guise or another; they are due to our human limits rather than particular situations. Let us not say, then, that things are harder today; they are simply different. But let us learn also from the saints who have gone before us, who confronted the difficulties of their own day. So I propose that we pause to rediscover some of the reasons which can help us to imitate them today. ... Loving others is a spiritual force drawing us to union with God.[39]

Chapter 5

LIVING IN A NEW
SPIRIT OF DIALOGUE
AND COOPERATION

In Jesus Christ, God became man: a man who sought others and was constantly in dialogue with them. He no longer stood unchangeable and immobile at the edge of the universe, the lonely origin of things, and it was no longer necessary to seek him outside of human history. He inserted himself into history, transforming it, working out our salvation, establishing his reign of justice and peace — his kingdom of love and peace — among mankind. The brothers of Tibhirine built their personal and communal lives on the gift of themselves. Such an interior generosity — which is precisely a response to a call — makes it possible for us to accept others who come into our lives, since "our lives are already a gift." We can only really live in dialogue and relation with others if we give up ourselves — if we lose ourselves — as Jesus says.

"Present in an Islamic land for more than forty years, I compare our mission to the morning star, which I like to contemplate when it rises in the heavens above Atlas. It shines joyfully, all alone in the obscure sky, announcing the coming of day. Among Muslims, we are those who shed light on the dialogue of friendship, signs that it is possible to meet others in the light of our faith in the one God," said Brother Jean-Pierre Schumacher, one of the Tibhirine Trappists who survived the tragedy. "We climb a ladder that ascends to the God who calls us, faithful to prayer, which is our means of communicating with Him."[40]

"Those who shed light on the dialogue of friendship, signs that it is possible to meet others" in mutual respect. The martyrs of Atlas open the road to Emmaus for us, where the love of God is manifested through human relationships, just as in the Gospel the two disciples recognized Christ risen from the dead after they walked and talked with him.

This journey is also, in the first place, the journey of the Visitation, which evokes the encounter between Mary and Elizabeth, where the virgin — after the historic annunciation of divine maternity — comes out of herself and goes to aid her elderly cousin who is about to give birth to the prophet John the Baptist.

"Elizabeth elicited Mary's *Magnificat*. If we fundamentally open ourselves and live our encounters with others in utter attention to them and a desire to connect with them, needing that other person's being and needing to hear what he has to say, then perhaps he will say something that pertains to us and what we are carrying inside, revealing to us how he takes part in whatever it is we are going through," wrote Christian de Chergé. "This makes it possible for us to prolong our participation in the Eucharist since the *Magnificat* we sing is, fundamentally, the Eucharist. The Church's first Eucharist was Mary's *Magnificat*."[41]

To sum up this beautiful message: Muslims, as bearers of God's message, reveal Christians to themselves, just as Elizabeth revealed Mary to herself.

The statue of Our Lady of Atlas, wearing a crown of twelve stars and sitting atop the monastery situated on Abd el-Kader, manifests the mystery of the Visitation: Mary is depicted as expecting a child, extending her hands toward all — Muslims and Christians — as she strives to mitigate the sorrows of the apocalypse, which are the "indifference, the veiled hate" that "breaks down the network of human relations." It is precisely these sufferings, these evils, that the monks wanted to assuage by using, both individually and collectively, the mystery of the cross, rooted in the Eucharist and the sacraments of the Church; the cross that is the "tree of life ... the leaves [of which] serve as medicine for the nations" (Rv 22:2).

"The temptation is always to find a reason to be at odds with others. Cain versus Abel, the Jews versus the pagans," Father Christian said in a homily on July 17, 1994, the feast of the first martyrs of North Africa. He quoted Lévinas in the same homily: "True brotherhood is the brotherhood that comes about because the other looks at me." He concluded, "The vocation of mankind is to unite. That is our way of being divine. And this can only occur if we — like Jesus — make ourselves a hostage to others, taking a step towards him."[42]

Our capacity to encounter others, to dialogue with them, is determined by the extent to which we can see that we too are "others," we too are "different" because of our religion. Deep within each one of us there is space for otherness, an interior capacity for accepting others precisely because we know that we too must be accepted. The brothers of Tibhirine chose to live this aspect of solidarity with others to the full, believing in the Holy Scriptures and in the singularity of Christ's disciples. Father Christophe treasured these encounters with others, recording his conversations with Muslim neighbors and, at the same time, staying in constant dialogue with Christ. In the autumn of 1994, for example, he wrote in his diary:

> While planting beans in the garden yesterday morning,
> Moussa said: "There is only one person in Algeria not
> trying to assume POWER: God. What God desires is
> man's wellbeing." He then turned to talk of a conviction
> that he has gradually convinced me of as well, something
> we can exchange ideas about: evil and viciousness are in
> the heart of every individual. I hear you speaking, you
> who know what is in the human heart.[43]

While the Tibhirine community was coming to grips with the
murder of religious men and women in Algeria, Father Christophe started a diary on May 8, 1994, after the funeral of Sister
Esther and Sister Caridad, both of whom were assassinated: "It
is our very vocation that is now targeted ... a vocation to meet
others, to serve them, to stand in a community of values and cultures, to participate in Algeria's future, and to work for the coming of faith."[44] One month later, he commented on another aspect
of their fraternal life that put them at risk as they worked on the
periphery of an area where everyone was welcomed without discrimination:

> Three well-armed men were received in the medical clinic yesterday evening. ... It was indeed You who came —
> sick — in these men: men bent on killing. Yes, they are
> sick in their hearts, which are sick with a desire to kill
> their brothers. But at the same time, what is really in *my*
> heart?[45]

This same spirit of openness we find in Father Célestin can be
found in all seven of the Atlas martyrs, including the doctor
Brother Luc, who with great wisdom wrote: "Salvation comes

from others who are the presence of God who calls us to life."[46]

Brother Luc, whom the Muslims called "Frélou," teaches us the meaning of long-suffering and patience with ourselves. He was sure of one thing:

"If faith saves, it is because it turns our gaze to the other and therefore creates a relationship that brings us out of our mortal loneliness."[47]

"Every time we lay aside self-interest for the good of another, we live this faith, which — even when we are unaware of it — is a faith in God, an attempt to give up our lives for Christ. ... If you want to be happy, make someone else happy. ... If he or she doesn't respond, it doesn't matter; it is in the act itself that we find life."[48]

For a long time, every day was "a book of signs" for Brother Luc, signs of "encounters," "contradictions," "difficulties," and "conversations."[49]

Born at the beginning of the First World War, Brother Luc studied medicine before entering military service in Morocco. He subsequently returned to his homeland, and during the Second World War, he took the place of a husband and father in a German prison, where he cared for Russian prisoners infected with typhus fever. After becoming a humble, non-ordained lay brother of the Abby of Aiguebelle, he was sent to Atlas in 1946, where he opened a medical dispensary that he managed until his death in 1996 at the age of eighty-two. His fidelity to the suffering local population was unshakable. Following in the footsteps of Padre Pio, he walked the way of poverty for years as the best way of encountering others. He cared for wounded rebels during the Algerian War, much to the chagrin of French officials.

The medical dispensary was always open to those who wanted to talk about their personal struggles and family difficulties, appreciating Brother Luc's wise advice. He put himself constantly at the service of Christ, because "we tend to love those who are dear to us simply in order to possess them for ourselves. And this is what we always must strive to free ourselves from."[50] Brother Luc teaches us to love others for their own sake, precisely because Jesus is present in them. "Jesus teaches us to meet him in another form in the life of each and every person. He is truly present in the human person. It is up to us to discover him there."[51] An image of Marthe Robin was found among his personal possessions. On the reverse was written: "Heaven is not for tomorrow or in ten years. It is something we can possess now if we are poor and crucified."

The violent death of the seven Trappist monks made clear to everyone the purity of their gospel message, lived fully in the years leading up to the tragedy. They have left the legacy of a holy, spiritual journey to be lived now. The path is enlightened by sharing the journey with those around us in trust and friendship.

"We like to speak of our encounters with non-Christians as 'sacramental,'" Henri Teissier, bishop emeritus of Algiers, explained during a symposium for European students in Santiago de Compostela in July 1999. He continued: "To live this 'sacrament of encounter,' we need 'sacrament-persons,' or rather persons who are signs and guardians of the gift God has made to each and every one of us, and that these persons themselves represent their gift of self to one another."

The Gospel, presenting us with encounters with Jesus, teaches and reveals to us what a "sacrament-person" is. Everyone is called to live this vocation today: the mission of Christ to go out to others. It is the art of encounter — of engaging in an encounter that is unforgettable, transformative, and contagious because it is lived in Christ.

To put an end to clericalism, a thorn in the Church's side, the blessed martyrs of Tibhirine, as well as Pope Francis, proposed a Church whose center of gravity is real people and society at large, rather than the Church's internal business. "A story of Christian witness has been written in Algeria and has contributed to an important evolution in the concept of 'mission,' not only in the Algerian Church but in the Catholic Church worldwide," Bishop Teissier said just two years after the death of the monks.[52]

In his personal notes, Brother Luc radically described this urgent transition to a less cumbersome, freer, and more purified Church, faithful to its origins:

> We need to pass through a phase of desperation if we want to arrive at a true relationship with God. We have to shed everything — our moral qualities, our virtues, our ecclesial structures, our doctrine — and truly pass through death if we want to unite ourselves with him. In this state of death and absolute desperation, one person alone will remain for us: Christ. If we truly turn to Him, we cannot help but open ourselves to Him! From that moment on a new type of existence begins: we can walk on water.[53]

As Pope Francis wrote:

> It means learning to find Jesus in the faces of others, in their voices, in their pleas. And learning to suffer in the embrace of the crucified Jesus whenever we are unjustly attacked or meet with ingratitude, never tiring of our decision to live in fraternity. There indeed we find true healing, since the way to relate to others which truly heals instead of debilitating us, is a mystical fraternity, a contemplative fraternity. It is a fraternal love capable of seeing the sacred grandeur of our neighbor, of finding God in every human being, of tolerating the nuisances of life in common by clinging to the love of God, of opening the heart to divine love and seeking the happiness of oth-

ers just as their heavenly Father does. .... Let us not allow ourselves to be robbed of community![54]

Chapter 6

ACCEPTING THE
UNEXPECTED WITH MARY

Insofar as they consecrate themselves to her at the moment of their solemn vows, Cistercians have a special devotion to Mary. They are deeply aware of how the Virgin Mary is the prime model of openness to the mystery of God, she who gives fullness to human life in Christ. Cistercians honor the Virgin of the Annunciation, who with her *fiat* opens herself to God without reserve, and the Virgin of the Assumption, who stands as the model for the full realization of the human person. Mary is a living model for our entire lives. Every evening, throughout the world, Cistercian men and women conclude their day by singing the *Salve Regina.* Mary is present in our "valley of tears" as "the Mother of Mercy." She shows us Christ, the Savior of all humanity.

The seven martyrs of Atlas were ready to accept the unpredictable, knowing that God is always present in the unexpected. Our yearning for his love spurs us on as he awaits the "yes" of friendship spontaneously and joyfully given.

Here is what Jean-Paul Vesco, who succeeded Pierre Claverie as bishop of Oran, had to say about the monks: "The truth about the Tibhirine martyrs is that they were driven one day to accept the extreme consequence of the gift of themselves for the sake of love."

We see that those who accept God's love — such as the biblical prophets Elijah, Jeremiah, and Hosea — open themselves up to a new adventure. Is it not the case that in the Gospel Jesus is constantly traveling as he calls others to follow him? Martyrdom — the greatest "yes" we can give — is prepared for by a lot of little "yeses" along the way. This is the way it was for the Virgin Mary, who is nothing but a "yes," a model for the Cistercian brothers of Atlas who follow in the footsteps of Saint Bernard, their patron, known as "Mary's cantor."

Father Christophe, the poet among the seven martyrs, eloquently expresses this spiritual bond with Mary in his diary. In May 1995, he wrote, "To see Mary ... in the shade of the Spirit, at the foot of the Cross, in the joy of Love, in her glorification ... to see Mary in the splendor of your divine plan, *Abba*: completely harmonized with your ineffable desire. I approach her. I accept from your Son my place among the disciples: Here I am. I come."[55] Today, just as then, in order to join Mary in accepting God's coming, we must make a radical conversion, opening our hearts to the unexpectedness of God, who can at times trouble us.

Ready to accept all trials and to hand over his very life, Christophe wrote: "The Spirit of truth comes. Mary was completely stunned at first. He tells us what must happen. It includes everything that must happen to us, bound up in Love-Event-Gift."[56]

"You, above all things, the Unexpected who reveals our thirst to us: Come. ... Vulnerable to the core ... we have been pierced with the same sword that pierced your heart and the heart of Mary, our refuge."[57]

Father Christophe, the youngest brother of the Tibhirine community, consecrated himself to Mary, "Mother of the crucified kiss and mercy poured out for us,"[58] on the feast of Saint Joseph, March 19, 1976, at the Abbey of Tamié, when he had already decided to leave for the Algerian monastery. Through this filial gift of himself, he desired to join himself fully to the Lord and rediscover the new life given to him at baptism. What he wanted to do most was sing Mary's *Magnificat* immersed in the love of his brothers, as the text of his consecration says:

> It was Joseph and Jesus who taught me your *Magnificat.*
> They sang it often in the workshop at Nazareth. ... You
> sang it to them so often! It was the way they expressed
> their love for you, with your own words welling up from
> the Spirit.

By consecrating ourselves to Mary, we deepen and purify our relationship with Christ so that we can discern more clearly what is essential to our lives. At the same time, Mary teaches us the action of grace in the marvels God works in our lives and leads us to adore the Son and to serve our neighbor. Mary leads us to pray for others, to contemplate Jesus, and to be docile to the Holy Spirit. Father Christophe renewed his consecration on March 19, 1996, so that he might become an "offering," as he writes in a prayer to Mary: "I receive you from the hands of Jesus along with the poor and sinners. With the Beloved Disciple, I take you into my home. My offering will be to stand by your side."[59] On the day of the assassination, he presided at the monastic Eucharist in the Chapel of the Little Sisters of Bab-el-Oued, where Sisters Esther and Caridad — as well as Brother Henry — had come so often to receive Communion. All three had been assassinated in Algiers in the previous months.

As violence spread with greater ferocity across Algeria, the prior, Father Christian, said, "You know, if something were to happen to us, not we but the people around us would be the real martyrs." He used to tell the story about two young brothers of a man who had fled into the woods who were tortured and killed on April 1, 1994. Their bodies, terribly mutilated, were given back to their father by the police with no further explanation other than that they were ordered to remain silent about it. This silence, the silence of the Passion, the silence of the greatest love, the silence of Jesus' total gift of himself, is also the silence and the hour of Mary. That hour when Mary was intimately united to the sacrifice of her Son as she stood under the cross. Contrary to the way she is often portrayed, Mary was neither prostrate nor swooning. Rather, she was standing on her own two feet because she lived intensely and completely with her Son, who sacrificed his life and poured out his blood for mankind. The brothers of Tibhirine also remained standing throughout those tragic years, under the cross, remaining in communion with the blood of so many innocent victims. In his homily on Good Friday in 1994, Father Christian recalled the innocent blood poured out on Calvary that allowed creation to "take its proper place in the divine innocence in which it once stood":

> Lost innocence can be restored. It has not been completely
> destroyed. It persists in the core of every human being. It
> exists at the foot of the cross and it awaits itself there. It has
> a name and a face: Mary, the new Eve. She is ready to bring
> us to the light once more. Everyone. Here is your mother,
> the dwelling place of my majesty, full of grace. [60]

The mother of Christ and of the Church will accompany the seven Trappists on their journey of the cross freely chosen as they sing their Paschal *Magnificat*. Abducted on the day after the Annunciation — the feast of Mary's "yes" — their remains were discovered on May 30, the vigil of the Visitation. At a conference in 2006, the abbot general of the Cistercians, Father Bernardo Olivera, explained the significance of the sacrifice of the Atlas martyrs as a *Via Mariae:*

> The mother of Jesus, our mother, constantly leads us to the Eucharist ... we can say that Mary lived her Eucharistic faith before the sacrament was instituted: at the moment of the Incarnation, "she offered her body" so that the Divine Word might become flesh in order to offer Himself as an immolation. We also know that when Jesus, referring to Calvary, said, "Do this in memory of me" (Lk 22:19), he was also referring to what his mother has done for us: here is your son, here is your mother. Whoever fully lives the Eucharist also accepts the mother and gives himself as a son.

A few days before Holy Week — at 1:15 a.m. in the dead of night — Brothers Christian, Luc, Christophe, Michel, Bruno, Célestin, and Paul were abducted. During the vigil celebration of the Eucharist in their chapel, the Gospel of John was read, in which Jesus announces his departure: "I am with you for a little while; but you will look for me."

If there was one monk who should not have been abducted with his brothers, it was Father Bruno. We now turn to consider his unique witness. Superior of the Moroccan monastic community of Fez, he had just arrived in Tibhirine to participate in the election of the prior. He had lived in Algeria as a child and loved the country and its people. His father had worked there as a career government official. When Bruno was of military age, he served under the Algerian flag for eighteen months before the War of Independence. He had backbone just like three of his companions — Christian, Paul, and Célestin — who, unlike Bruno, fought on the French side.

Bruno was deeply touched by the Salesian Sisters of Don Bosco, who had an enormous influence on his relationship to the Eucharist. We are called to follow Christ and, with him, to place ourselves at the service of the salvation of humankind. It is precisely in the Eucharist that we celebrate, contemplate, and find the nourishment, the grace, and the strength to live as witnesses to Christ and proclaim him boldly. Mary accordingly assumes the role of teacher in this. She invites us to accept the unexpected in our lives, to let ourselves be shaken out of slumber, to make progress in our earthly pilgrimage. The Salesian Sisters also instilled a love of radical poverty in Bruno. When he became a monk at Bellefontaine, the call to radical and fruitful material poverty resonated with him: "There is no real spiritual poverty without real material poverty," he said as he set out for Atlas. "My one goal is to bring the prayer of Jesus into this land, in the spirit of Father de Foucauld," he later confessed.

Father Bruno was a man who lived the hidden life of Nazareth. During his pilgrimage to the Holy Land, he was deeply affected by the unforgettable moment when he visited the chapel of the Little Sisters of Jesus of Nazareth and knelt in the very place where Father Charles de Foucauld passed countless hours in prayer.[61] With Bruno, we can take a true look at the place we give to prayer, simplicity, and silence in our lives. During his hidden life in Nazareth, Jesus remained in the silence of ordinary existence. He has thus given us the opportunity to live in communion with him in the holiness of a daily life marked by prayer, simplicity, exhaustion, and love lived in community with a family.

Father Bruno had passionately sought out his vocation, and he finally found it in humble life, a life of work where one can retreat a bit and live in union with God while remaining intimately tied to his fellow men. For Bruno, Algeria was "a little desert in the land of Islam where a few brothers helped one another mutually to live the life of the Gospel of Jesus."[62] But the unexpected was sprung upon him when he was sent to be superior of the small monastic foundation at Fez in Morocco, where he strove to live the small details of everyday life in the spirit of Jesus, Mary, and Joseph.

In accepting the sudden turn of events on the night between March 26 and 27, 1996, he put into practice the prayer of abandonment that guided Father de Foucauld's footsteps for many years: "Father, I abandon myself to you. ... I am ready for anything, I accept everything so that your will may be accomplished in me and in all your creatures." Bruno had a deep Marian devotion, so he repeated this prayer — which he had learned in his youth — throughout the day: "May the Father and the Son and the Holy Spirit be glorified in every place by the Immaculate Virgin Mary."

To the Tibhirine brothers, it was virtually unthinkable that they flee the impending risk that weighed upon them for months. They accepted everything, even this risk, as something from the hands of God. It is most likely that the greatest factor in their decision to stay was the unshakable courage of the oldest among them, Brother Luc, the eighty-two-year-old "little doctor" whom everyone admired deeply and had the greatest respect for. Constantly solicitous for the poor and the sick, even while struggling with his own heart and lung problems, he showed an immense trust in God and "blind hope."[63]

This hope, shared by each of his brothers, is our hope too. We know with certainty that Christ is risen, that death has no power over him, and that he desires to share eternal life with us so that we may join him in reigning victorious over death and enjoying eternal life with him in a mysterious, unspeakable way. To return to God — this was Brother Luc's ever-burning desire.

> For Jesus, the end of the road is God. Similarly, our journey — through the resurrection — is to God. The resurrection occurs inside of us every day in the midst of

sadness and suffering. If every love is a dying to oneself in order to live for others, to love means to learn to die in order to live.[64]

Just like Brother Luc, the monks of Tibhirine knew that their death could be a witness to God's absoluteness. Father Christophe sheds light on this conviction: "You know well that I feel more and more involved in what Algeria is going through, in the violence and deadly lies it is suffering. The only thing that can stop all of this is the greatest act of love: the cross." With a heart open to surprises and the unexpected, Christophe saw Mary "in the joy of love," and with her the seven martyrs were glorified.

As Pope Francis wrote:

Faith also means believing in God, believing that he truly loves us, that he is alive, that he is mysteriously capable of intervening, that he does not abandon us and that he brings good out of evil by his power and his infinite creativity. It means believing that he marches triumphantly in history with those who "are called and chosen and faithful" (Rv 17:14). Let us believe the Gospel when it tells us that the kingdom of God is already present in this world and is growing, here and there, and in different ways: like the small seed which grows into a great tree (cf. Mt 13:31–32), like the measure of leaven that makes the dough rise (cf. Mt 13:33) and like the good seed that grows amid the weeds (cf. Mt 13:24–30) and can always pleasantly surprise us. The kingdom is here, it returns, it struggles to flourish anew. Christ's resurrection everywhere calls forth seeds of that new world; even if they are cut back, they grow again, for the resurrection is already secretly woven into the fabric of this history, for Jesus did not rise in vain. May we never remain on the sidelines of this march of living hope! Because we do not always see these seeds growing, we need an interior certainty, a conviction that God is able to act in every situation, even amid apparent setbacks.[65]

Chapter 7

GUESTS IN THE
HOUSE OF ISLAM

"Guests of the Algerian people — in a thoroughly Islamic country — these brothers wanted to do their part to show that peace between peoples is a gift from God in every place and at every time, and that it is up to believers — both now and then — to manifest this inalienable gift, especially through the quality of their mutual respect and their concerted effort to support a healthy and fruitful spiritual exchange."[66]

Since there is a constant need to discover new ways of cultivating and fostering a genuine relationship between Christians and Muslims, the deplorable deaths of the Tibhirine monks nonetheless serve as an inspiration for the choices we make. The "silent presence" of Tibhirine has become a "universal word": a friendly and brotherly welcome that lived in the hope that others would extend a friendly and brotherly welcome in return; an encounter with others that took root in the everyday; a living, intercultural, and interreligious dialogue put into practice through an exchange of gifts that allowed everyone to affirm their own identity.

Like Blessed Charles de Foucauld, the prior of Tibhirine was convinced that, if we truly want to understand Muslims, we must live among them not only face-to-face, but shoulder-to-shoulder, venerating the one God in friendship and prayer. He believed that the place of Islam in God's overall plan was a "tricky question." "I'll have an answer for that only after I die," he said, confident in the "reminders of the Gospel values nourished by the Muslim faith." Abbot Christian used to read the Koran in Arabic, even using it for *lectio divina,* without, of course, giving in to syncretism, but rather searching for those "hidden, underground waters of grace"[67] that benefited Muslims as well. He was fond of clarifying this spiritual search for unity by referring to an ongoing dialogue he had with a young man who often visited the monastery: "If we dug a well in the middle of the monastery, would the water found there be Christian or Muslim?" It would be "God's water,"[68] the young man responded.

Together with Father Claude Rault — who would later become the bishop of Laghouat in the Sahara — Abbot Christian came up with the idea of creating an interreligious dialogue group. The two men were not alone in their desire to cultivate lasting friendly relations with Muslims. They established the group with the name *Ribat es Salam,* which in Arabic means "bond of peace," in 1979, long before the monks were assassinated. This allowed the monks at Tibhirine to host discussions on a theme dear to their hearts as they brought together Christians and Muslims in day-to-day living.

On the night the monks were abducted, some members of the Islamic-Christian dialogue group were staying at the monastery. "It was as if *Ribat* had been entrusted with the mission of representing the Algerian people while they accompanied the monks in their suffering," said Anne-Noëlle Clement.[69]

In a common search for God, men and women in *Ribat* were united in their desire for communion, remembering a time of old when Jews, Christians, and Muslims lived in mutual respect, especially in Andalusia and Morocco. This "Córdoba Islam" is often considered the true Islam of Algeria, particularly in the area of Atlas in which Tibhirine is located, which was the geographical center of the Abd-el-Kader Emirate until its destruction in 1847.

In this historically complex region, a small group of Sufi Muslims, followers of Sheikh Bentounès, would gather with Christians — including Father Christian, Brother Michel, and Father Christophe — twice a year in Tibhirine in order to dialogue, listen, and sing together, asserting friendship as their chief mission. So as not to confuse the different religious traditions and practices, the meetings of *Ribat* never took place in the monastery chapel, but rather in the guesthouse. *Alawiyya* Muslims in Medea, who were inspired by Sufi mysticism, had proposed from the beginning that the participants would not focus primarily on dogmatic discussions, but would rather "allow God to create something new ... in prayer," as Father Christian reported during a conference in Rome in 1989.

According to Father Christian, dialogue must go beyond words and lead to authentic spiritual communion. To explain this, he used the image of Jacob's ladder in a way similar to Saint Benedict's use of it in the chapter on "Humility" in his *Rule*. There he describes the spiritual journey of a monk in terms of climbing a set of stairs or a ladder. For Father Christian, this could take the form of a "spiritual ladder." The two rails of the ladder represent the Christian and Muslim faiths. The legs are firmly planted in the ground — that is, the earth shared by all human beings — while the ladder rises up to heaven. This is the ascent proposed to us: to climb together toward our final end to encounter God. It is through dialogue — a dialogue about the spiritual life and the daily living of every human being — that we are able to enter into a communion that does not deny differences, but rather points to a future of hope.

Over the course of time, through the experience of the *Ribat*, Muslims and Christians together climbed both rungs of the ladder, growing closer to one another as they approached God together. "There are corresponding points between the pillars of Islam and the essential practices of every form of consecrated life. We can view them as poles of a common ascent,"[70] Father Christian explained in his description of this "mystical ladder of dialogue":

> The rung of a ladder is firmly inserted into each of the two rails, and — hopefully! — at the same height. When we try to define these levels of authentic spiritual progress, we are surprised to find that they are so close to one another.[71]

The prior of Tibhirine went on to describe the various rungs of the ladder that Christians and Muslims climb together, each faithful to its own tradition and without confusion:

> The gift of oneself to the All-Powerful God, regular prayer, fasting, almsgiving, conversion of the heart, mindfulness of God or *dhikr*, trust in divine providence, welcoming others without boundaries, the call to spiritual battle, pilgrimage (which can also be internal), and so on.

In all of this, Father Christian recognized the Spirit of holiness, the Spirit whose origin and destination remains a mystery to everyone (cf. Jn 3:8), emphasizing that its purpose is always to give birth from on high (Jn 3:7) and to attract us to the way of ascension — a reciprocal conversion in which God strives to get us gradually involved (one rung at a time), in proportion to our fidelity, until the definitive coming of his kingdom. The monks of Tibhirine were convinced that Islamic-Christian dialogue, if it lives in truth and with respect for the faith of the other, can be a journey of reciprocal imitation. This journey urges us to promote the quality of the human dimension, because this is an opening to otherness, to fight the good fight for the respect of life and justice, to be attentive to the most disadvantaged of our brothers.

Six of the nineteen beatified Algerian martyrs were members of *Ribat* (the three brothers of Tibhirine already mentioned, together with Henri Vergès, Christian Chessel, and Sister Odette). They strove to put the spiritual and fraternal ideal into practice together with the Algerian people. One of the main factors influencing the ecumenical path undertaken at Tibhirine, a path we too are called to follow, was the unforgettable encounter Christian de Chergé had when serving as a second lieutenant in the Algerian war. Charged with managing the refugee camp near Tiaret, he formed a close friendship with one of the camp guards named Mohammed, a deeply religious man who "had liberated" Christian's faith and taught him to live in simplicity, openness, and abandonment to God.

"Our dialogue was one of peaceful friendship based on a mutual trust in God's will that transcended the surrounding chaos,"[72] Father Christian recalled, remembering that his monastic vocation in Algeria was rooted in his loyalty to the friendship — sealed in blood — that he had with his "friend who had gone before him." Mohammed was assassinated near the local well by members of the National Liberation Army (ALN) who were fighting for the country's independence from France. He had given his life like so many other Muslims who remained loyal to France.

Father Christian describes the events that launched his decision to pursue the path to religious life:

That illiterate man was never happy with pretty but empty words. Incapable of betraying his brothers and friends, he risked his life despite the burden it would be to his ten children. When a fight broke out between his brother Muslims, he expressed this gift concretely by protecting a friend who was more vulnerable than he was. Conscious of the threat surrounding him, he accepted the humble promise to "pray for him." His only response was, "I know that you will pray for me ... but look, Christians don't know how to pray." I took his words as a reproach against the Church who, at least at that time, was not presenting herself as a community of prayer.[73]

Referring to the death of Mohammed, killed for retaliation against his brother Muslims, the prior of Tibhirine furnished the basic elements of the great undertaking in which he had involved so many men and women:

From the blood of my friend, I recognized that my call to follow Christ was destined to be lived — sooner or later — in the same country in which this greatest pledge of love was given to me. I became aware, at the same time, that this consecration of my life had to pass through a common prayer if it was to be truly a witness to the Church.[74]

In Father Christian's eyes, Mohammed's martyrdom was eucharistic, in the sense that he had made a gift of himself. He had always considered his friend a martyr in the literal sense of the word — that is, as a "witness" of love. This was the key to understanding Father Christian's life in Algeria and his desire to understand Islam. This can also help our own desire to deepen our spiritual life by seeking to better understand that which our faith in Jesus can accept from the experience of other religions. We can recall the words of Pope Saint John Paul II during a trip to Morocco in 1985:

> Man is a *spiritual being*. We, believers, know that we do not live in a closed world. We believe in God. We are worshippers of God. We are seekers of God. The Catholic Church regards with respect and *recognizes the quality of your religious progress*, the richness of your spiritual tradition. We Christians, also, are proud of our own religious tradition. I believe that we, Christians and Muslims, must recognize with joy the religious values that we have in common, and give thanks to God for them. Both of us believe in one God the only God, who is all Justice and all Mercy; we believe in the importance of prayer, of fasting, of almsgiving, of repentance and of pardon; we believe that God will be a merciful judge to us at the end of time, and we hope that after the resurrection he will be satisfied with us and we know that we will be satisfied with him.[75]

Father Christian — who arrived in Tibhirine in 1971 at the age of thirty-four — acknowledged these common values with joy, and he would keep the promise he made to Mohammed when the latter gave his own life. Father Christian recognized Christ's own self-gift in Mohammed's death, and this was the basis for his efforts to strengthen the bonds between the monks and the Muslim population through the invocation of the Holy Spirit, "the gift whose secret joy will always be to create communion by playing with differences."[76]

From the time of his youth, spent with his parents in Algeria, he knew that "the God of Islam and the God of Jesus Christ are not two divinities."[77] At that time, his mother was already teaching him, from the age of five, a respect for the correct way Muslims were praying.

There were those who accused Father Christian of compromising his Christian faith through his close relationship with Islam. But he looked beyond this, convinced that the spiritual life of Muslims could give its own special contribution not only to a better Christian understanding of God, but also the way that they could be in a daily, permanent relationship with him. "Fortunately, there are people who know how to live in a way that goes beyond the mere appearance of things,"[78] Archbishop Teissier once said when commenting on the daring positions advanced by the prior of Atlas. The archbishop praised his battle for a disarmed brotherhood and "a genuine evangelical implementation of the Paschal mystery."

Together with his brother monks, Father Christian believed that mercy, something of infinite value to Muslims, was "the seal of the covenant that God made with creation," and that they should therefore "immediately multiply the sources of mercy," such as the source found at Tibhirine. To accomplish this, they had "to logically renounce any pretense of superiority" and "to understand together that God calls us to humility."[79]

Thus, mercy and humility would be the key ideas offered by the martyrs of Tibhirine to the Church and her efforts at interreligious dialogue geared toward building bridges with adherents of Islam in service to the brotherhood willed by God, Creator and Father of all. The suffering these monks endured and the mystery of their disappearance are the birth pains for bringing forth a new humanity. What really counts is that, in a world torn asunder, we can respond to the call of these men to speak with nonviolent words and treat one another with disarming love.

The fact that these seven martyrs were living in a foreign land confers a universal dimension to the path of dialogue they undertook side-by-side with their Muslim neighbors, which is all the more the case given that the obscure circumstances surrounding their assassination suggest that the crime against them had nothing to do with Islam. "I am well aware of the characteristics of Islam that could lead to a sort of Islamism. It is too easy to pacify our conscience by equating this religious way with distortions created by extremists," Father Christian wrote in his testament, pardoning his assassin ahead of time, alluding to him as his "last-minute friend."[80] "You too, my last-minute friend, knew not what you were doing. Yes, for you too I wish this GRACE, this *AD-DIO* ("until God"). O blessed thieves, may God, our Father, grant that we meet one another again in heaven. AMEN! *Inch'Allah!*"

As Pope Francis has written:

> The sacred writings of Islam have retained some Christian teachings; Jesus and Mary receive profound veneration and it is admirable to see how Muslims both young and old, men and women, make time for daily prayer and faithfully take part in religious services. Many of them also have a deep conviction that their life, in its entirety, is from God and for God. They also acknowledge the need to respond to God with an ethical commitment and with mercy towards those most in need. ... Faced with disconcerting episodes of violent fundamentalism, our respect for true followers of Islam should lead us to avoid hateful generalizations, for authentic Islam and the proper reading of the Koran are opposed to every form of violence.[81]

APPENDIX 1

Spiritual Testimony of Father Christian

Facing a GOODBYE ...

If it should happen one day — and it could be today — that I become a victim of the terrorism which now seems ready to engulf all the foreigners living in Algeria, I would like my community, my Church, and my family to remember that my life was GIVEN to God and to this country.

I ask them to accept the fact that the One Master of all life was not a stranger to this brutal departure.

I would ask them to pray for me: For how could I be found worthy of such an offering?

I ask them to associate this death with so many other equally violent ones which are forgotten through indifference or anonymity.

My life has no more value than any other. Nor any less value. In any case, it has not the innocence of childhood.

I have lived long enough to know that I am an accomplice in the evil that seems to prevail so terribly in the world, even in the evil that might blindly strike me down.

I should like, when the time comes, to have a moment of spiritual clarity which would allow me to beg forgiveness of God and of my fellow human beings, and at the same time forgive with all my heart the one who would strike me down.

I could not desire such a death. It seems to me important to state this.

I do not see, in fact, how I could rejoice if the people I love were indiscriminately accused of my murder.

It would be too high a price to pay for what will perhaps be called the "grace of martyrdom," to owe it to an Algerian, whoever he might be, especially if he says he is acting in fidelity to what he believes to be Islam.

I am aware of the scorn that can be heaped on the Algerians indiscriminately.

I am also aware of the caricatures of Islam that a certain Islamism fosters.

It is too easy to soothe one's conscience by identifying this religious way with the fundamentalist ideology of its extremists.

For me, Algeria and Islam are something different: It is a body and a soul.

I have proclaimed this often enough, I think, in the light of what I have received from it.

I so often find there that true strand of the Gospel that I learned at my mother's knee, my very first Church, precisely in Algeria, and already inspired with respect for Muslim believers.

Obviously, my death will appear to confirm those who hastily judged me naive or idealistic: "Let him tell us now what he thinks of his ideals!"

But these persons should know that finally my most avid curiosity will be set free.

This is what I shall be able to do, God willing: immerse my gaze in that of the Father to contemplate with him his children of Islam just as he sees them, all shining with the glory of Christ, the fruit of his Passion, filled with the Gift of the Spirit whose secret joy will always be to establish communion and restore the likeness, playing with the differences.

For this life lost, totally mine and totally theirs, I thank God, who seems to have willed it entirely for the sake of that JOY in everything and in spite of everything.

In this THANK YOU, which is said for everything in my life from now on, I certainly include you, friends of yesterday and today, and you, my friends of this place, along with my mother and father, my sisters and brothers and their families — you are the hundredfold granted as was promised!

And also you, my last-minute friend, who will not have known what you were doing:

Yes, I want this THANK YOU and this GOODBYE to be a "GOD BLESS" for you, too, because in God's face I see yours.

May we meet again as happy thieves in Paradise, if it please God, the Father of us both.

AMEN! *INCH'ALLAH!*
Algiers, December 1, 1993
Tibhirine, January 1, 1994

Christian +

APPENDIX 2

The Spirit of Tibhirine Is Alive

(Interview with Brother Jean-Pierre Schumacher)

Brother Jean-Pierre was responsible for the management of the guesthouse at the Trappist Monastery at Tibhirine at the time of the assassinations. He was one of only two survivors in 1996. The other was Brother Amadeus (who died in 2008). Brother Jean-Pierre continues to live the religious life at the monastery in Midelt, Morocco, south of Fez, in the small community of Our Lady of Atlas, "Kasbah Myriem." This is the community that succeeded Tibhirine in the Maghreb.

Brother Jean-Paul, how did your monastic life in Algeria begin?

I am from Lorraine. I was born in the department of Moselle on February 15, 1924. I wanted to be a priest since I was a boy because of the example set by my pastor. I accompanied him everywhere, especially on the roads as he would go to administer sacraments to those who lived alone. I received my formation from the Marists in a school on the French border. My father was a miller, so I learned his trade and practiced it until the outbreak of the war. Then I was obliged to enlist with the German army. Thanks to my weak health, I avoided deployment to the Russian front. I could have died in Stalingrad just like one of my good friends whose letters I have carefully preserved. As a young man, I made the decision to enter the religious life while praying in the Chapel of Our Lady in the Cathedral of Senlis. I was ordained a Marist priest in 1953. I later heard of the Trappist monastery at "Tibharine" (that was how it was being pronounced at the time) in Algeria. The call resonated deep in my soul. In 1957, I obtained the authorization of my superiors to enter the Trappist monastery at Timadeuc, where I made my solemn profession on August 20, 1960, awaiting my departure for Algeria, which finally occurred in 1964 at the request of Cardinal Duval, archbishop of Algiers. The bugs, the dogs, the heat — all of this was difficult, and the atmosphere was tense after Algeria declared independence. It was indeed a difficult historical time for everyone.

What was life like among the Algerian Muslims before the rise of armed Islamists and the reality of civil war — that is, in the years when the existence of the community at Tibhirine was virtually unknown?

Luc, the much-beloved doctor who constantly looked after the medical needs of the locals, and Amadeus were the only two religious members who had been associated with "Tibharine" for a long time. The others were sent there by their respective monastic communities to rebuild the abbey in the spirit of interreligious dialogue characterized by Vatican II. Our community lacked unity due to our diverse backgrounds. It was only in 1976 that we were able to elect a superior according to the procedures and norms of canon law. From that point on, our monastic community was strengthened by our common vow of stability as we dedicated ourselves to the path of "constancy," a word used by Cardinal

Duval, our common father. Christian, who had arrived in 1971, was elected to lead the community in 1984. We learned Arabic and recited the Our Father together in it. Our Muslim neighbors were our friends. We really became family with them as each side respected the religious traditions of the other.

What did you see or hear on the night of the abduction? What are your memories?
Beginning in 1993, armed Islamists — our "brothers in the mountains" — often came to the monastery at night searching for medicine and medical supplies. We remained neutral in the conflict between the rebels and the Algerian military. Just like during the Algerian War, Luc administered medical care to the "rebels" in the name of Christ's love for all the suffering. The authorities did not understand our attitude. A group came to abduct the monks on March 27, 1996, perhaps with the intention of taking them away but not killing them. What happened after that? One day perhaps we will find out. What I can say with certainty about that terrible night is that the armed men who came were not behaving normally. They did not knock before coming in as they usually did when looking for Luc, our doctor. They took my seven brothers, including Bruno, who had just arrived from Morocco, and they just left. The Muslim guard of the monastery courageously refrained from giving out information and practically "forgot" about two of the monks: Amadeus, who had locked his room, and myself, who had watched their sinister movements from my window and was unable to intervene. The telephone lines were cut. I prayed my brothers would be witnesses of God's goodness to these mysterious abductors. At the very least, they were messengers of peace.

Why did you come to Morocco?
Our monastery had founded a small monastic community in Fez, Morocco, in 1988. Bruno, one of our brothers at Fez, gave his life

in my place at the moment of the abduction. He was taken by mistake, because he was only a temporary guest at Tibhirine. Before I learned that the seven brothers were dead, I went to Fez in May of 1996 with Brother Amadeus so we could continue our Christian duty of praying as pilgrims of friendship in a Muslim world. Since I was elected prior of the community at Fez, I stayed in Morocco to participate in the installation ceremony at the monastery further south, at Midelt, in the mountains around Atlas where Tibhirine is located, the only mountain chain connecting the Maghreb with the outlying area. Our Lady of Atlas, in Morocco, had by that time taken the place of the community in Algeria. Today there is another Jean-Pierre, Father Flachaire, in charge of our small community in Midelt, and we are faithfully awaiting the arrival of other brothers. The spirit of Tibhirine is alive. Come and see!

Why is your Christian presence in Morocco, an ocean of Islam, important today?
We've already been present in this Muslim territory for more than fifty years. Our presence is often compared to the morning star, a sight I often contemplated in the skies above Atlas. Venus burns brightly, all alone in the gray-black night, announcing that dawn is on its way. Living among Muslims, we are those who enlighten the dialogue of friendship. We are signs of an encounter made possible by the light of faith in the one God. We are ascending the two rails of the same ladder towards the God who calls us. We are faithful to prayer, a means of communication connecting us to God. In Morocco, we drink tea with our neighbors every day, and this reminds us of the Eucharistic chalice, a meeting of hearts, the value of which is beyond our capacity to calculate.

What is the secret to the friendly relations you have with the Muslims you live in the midst of?
Prayer. In Tibhirine, the bells of the monastery rang out calling

us to each hour of prayer, and the Muslims never once asked us to silence them. We have a mutual respect in our hearts for our common vocation: to adore God, to praise him, to sing his glory. In Morocco, we live this communion of prayer when we get up at night to pray at the same hour our Muslim neighbors do when they hear the muezzin. Faithfulness to the hours of prayer is the secret to our friendship with the Muslims. We join them in our desire to place ourselves in God's presence and our desire to be honest with the Light burning within us that we can only discover in silence. Our Muslim neighbors teach us how to pray. Like Charles de Foucauld, we take our example from them. Our Christian uniqueness consists in our belief that God gives us his Spirit and makes us partakers of his own life. This is the thrust of our witness.

What will you say to your brothers when you meet them in the next life?
There is no way their message can be expressed in political terms. To do so would be to ruin it. They gave their lives because of their love for a people. That is a big deal. A really big deal. When I heard of their deaths in Fez in May of 1996, I wanted to remember them worthily by wearing red vestments at Mass, the color of martyrs, as a way of rendering them thanks for the lives they led. They witnessed to the light and reincarnated the vocation of John the Baptist by preparing the way of the Lord on the threshold of the new millennium ... when we meet again in heaven, we will throw ourselves into each other's arms, happy we had loved and lived our gift of self to the end. I will especially thank my brother Luc for intervening so often, even after his death, as many of my Muslim friends will attest. Some say they have seen him miraculously appear to them in times of sickness.

Interviewed by François Vayne (in Morocco)

NOTES

[1] This expression is a literal translation of a liturgical prayer (*"pour la gloire de Dieu et le salut du monde"*) at the end of the Rite of Presentation of the Gifts at Mass. The current English translation is: "May the Lord accept the sacrifice at your hands, for the praise and glory of his name, for our good, and the good of all his Church."

[2] Christophe Lebreton, *Il soffio del dono: diario di fratel Christophe, monaco di Tibhirine* (Padua: EMP, 2001), 42.

[3] Christian de Chergé, *Dieu pour tout jour* (Godewaersvelde: Bellefontaine, 2004), 432.

[4] Christian de Chergé, *L'invincible espérance* (Montrouge: Bayard, 1997), 304.

[5] Christian de Chergé and the Community of Tibhirine, *Più forti dell'odio* (Magnano: Qiqajon, 2010), 28.

[6] Masson, *Tibhirine*, 109.

[7] de Chergé, *L'invincible espérance*, 50.

[8] Christian de Chergé, *Meditazioni sul Cantico dei Catici*, ed. Christian Salenson (Padua: EMP, 2016), 127.

[9] Monks of Tibhirine, *Heureux ceux qui espèrent*, 172.

[10] Ibid., 178.

[11] Cf. Francis, *Evangelii Gaudium*, 283.

[12] *Rule of Saint Benedict*, XLVIII, 8.

[13]Lebreton, *Il soffio,* 36.

[14]Ibid., 97.

[15]Bernard Gorce, "L'histoire des moines de Tibhirine," *La Croix,* September 5, 2010.

[16]de Chergé, *Dieu pour tout jour,* 330.

[17]Christophe Henning, *Méditer avec les moines de Tibhirine* (Paris: Salvator, 2015), 125.

[18]de Chergé, *Dieu pour tout jour,* 450.

[19]Brother Alberic was the religious name of Charles de Foucauld during his time with the Cistercian Order.

[20]Lebreton, *Il soffio,* 109.

[21]Monks of Tibhirine, *Heureux ceux qui espèrent,* 586.

[22]Lebreton, *Il soffio,* 119.

[23]Ibid., 205. This translation of the psalm is taken from *The New American Bible, Revised Edition,* used by the United States Conference of Catholic Bishops.

[24]Christine Ray, *Le cardinal Duval,* XX.

[25]Francis, *Evangelii Gaudium,* 279.

[26]Minassian, *Frère Christophe Lebreton,* 168.

[27]de Chergé, *Dieu pour tout jour,* 448.

[28]Ibid., 448.

[29]Ali Benhadjar, "The Islamic League for *dawa* and *jihad,*" a declaration, July 17, 1997.

[30]Interview with *Le Figaro,* February 6, 2011.

[31]de Chergé, *L'invincible espérance,* 310.

[32]Ibid., 296–97.

[33]Ibid., 297–98.

[34]Lebreton, *Il soffio,* 113.

[35]Pierre Claverie and the Bishops of the Maghreb, *Le livre de la foi: révélation et parole de Dieu dans la tradition chrétienne* (Paris: Cerf, 1996), 139.

[36]de Chergé, *L'invincible espérance,* 221. The entire text of Father Christian's testament can be found in appendix 1 of this book.

[37]Monks of Tibhirine, *Heureux ceux qui espèrent*, 296.

[38]Lebreton, *Il soffio*, 186.

[39]Francis, *Evangelii Gaudium*, 263 and 272.

[40]François Vayne, "L'esprit de Tibhirine est vivant: Rencontre avec le frère Jean-Pierre Schumacher," *La Vie, Les Essentiels*, April 2006. The complete text can be found in appendix 1 of this book.

[41]de Chergé, *Meditazioni sul Cantico*, 97.

[42]de Chergé, *L'autre que nous attendons*, 436–37.

[43]Lebreton, *Il soffio*, 112.

[44]Ibid., 117.

[45]Ibid., 119.

[46]Cf. Thomas Georgeon, "La transparence de l'absolu: Frère Luc, moine martyr de Tibhirine," *Collectanea Cisterciensia*, Vol. 69 (2007), 202–25.

[47]Ibid., 213.

[48]Ibid., 212.

[49]Ibid., 213.

[50]Ibid.

[51]Thomas Georgeon and Christophe Henning, *Frère Luc*, 184.

[52]*Cahiers de l'Orient*, 51 (1998).

[53]Georgeon, "La transparence de l'absolu," 215.

[54]Francis, *Evangelii Gaudium*, 91–92.

[55]Lebreton, *Il soffio*, 155.

[56]Ibid.

[57]Ibid., 31.

[58]Monks of Tibhirine, *Heureux ceux qui espèrent*, 531.

[59]Lebreton, *Il soffio*, 205.

[60]de Chergé, *L'autre que nous attendons*, 423–24.

[61]Monks of Tibhirine, *Heureux ceux qui espèrent*, 213.

[62]Ibid., 234.

[63]Georgeon, "La transparence de l'absolu," 222.

[64]Ibid.

[65]Francis, *Evangelii Gaudium*, 278–79.

[66]A passage from the introductory brochure for guests of the monastery

of Tibhirine.

[67]Louis Massignon, *Badaliya, au nom de l'autre (1947–1962)*, ed. Maurice Borrmans and Françoise Jacquin (Paris: Editions du Cerf, 2011), 398.

[68]Christian de Chergé and the Tibhirine Community, *Più forti dell'odio*, ed. Guido Dotti (Magnano: Qiqajon, 2006), 71.

[69]Anne-Noëlle Clément, *Le Verbe s'est fait frère* (Montrouge: Bayard, 2010), 34.

[70]de Chergé and the Tibhirine Community, *Più forti dell'odio*, 67.

[71]Christian de Chergé, "Comunicazione alle giornate romane," *Bollettino "Pro Dialogo"* of the Pontifical Council for Interreligious Dialogue, 73 (1990/1991).

[72]Robert Masson, *Jusqu'au bout de la nuit: l'Église d'Algérie* (Paris: CERF, 1998), 160.

[73]Ibid.

[74]Christian Salenson, *Prier 15 jours avec Christian de Chergé: Prieur des moines de Tibhirine* (Cork: Primento Digital Publishing, 2018) 47.

[75]John Paul II, "Address of His Holiness John Paul II to Young Muslims (August 19, 1985)" accessed August 10, 2020 , Vatican.va, par. 10.

[76]Christian de Chergé, *Spiritual Testament*. For the complete text, see the appendix of this book.

[77]"Lettera à Maurice Borrmans," *Islamochristiana*, 22 (1996): 6.

[78]Martine de Sauto, "Dossier," *La Croix*, December 31, 2005–January 1, 2006.

[79]de Chergé, "Comunicazione alle giornate romane."

[80]de Chergé, *Spiritual Testament* (see appendix 1).

[81]Francis, *Evangelii Gaudium*, 252–53.